THE BUSINESS

SECURITY K-9

THE BUSINESS
SECURITY K-9

Selection and Training

KAREN FREEMAN DUET
AND GEORGE DUET

HOWELL
BOOK
HOUSE

Macmillan•USA

Howell Book House
A Simon & Schuster Macmillan Company
15 Columbus Circle
New York, NY 10023

Library of Congress Cataloging-in-Publication Data available
ISBN 0-87605-439-4

Manufactured in the United States of America

10 9 8 7 6 5 4 3 2 1

To our teachers and our students,
all of whom have taught us many things,
and to our family for their
never-ending love and support.

The canine training techniques described in this book are intended for stable canine temperaments only and are not intended for any canine whose genetic or environmental lineage has been specially bred for unlawful or illegal purposes. All training techniques described in this book are proven methods of normal training developed over long periods of time, proved safe and efficient by recognized canine training experts. Neither the Authors nor the Publisher shall be liable for any claim, made by any person, trainer or owner, which arises out of the use or implementation of the various training methods contained in this book.

ACKNOWLEDGMENTS

K-9 Companions Dog Trainers and Associate Trainers:
Lisa Spadt (and Baby Teresa)
Dawn Gardner and Scott Gardner (Kennel Master, March AFB)
Bill Dingwell
Jim Kellerman and Darlene Kellerman
Bonnie Price and Doug Price
Steve Scheratis (Security Force Unlimited)
Steve Trachta (Security Force Unlimited)
Photographer: David Macias
Artist: Andrea Churches
Editorial helpers: Terri Struxness, Bonnie Price, Vern Freeman and Jerre Freeman
Breeders: Special thanks to Bonnie Price for arranging for such an exceptional group of breeders, Doug and Bonnie Price—Windeville Rottweilers, David Macias—Rosenholz German Shepherd Dogs, Daniele Daugherty—Crocs-Blancs Belgian Malinois, Linda Calamia—Aldercrest Doberman Pinschers, Sylvia

Hammarstrom—Skansen Giant Schnauzers, Dara Wilcox—Daradan Belgian Tervurens, Margi Roberson—Heleva Boxers, Jim and Edie Richards—Roderic Bullmastiffs, Wendy Norris Williams—Norris Place Dogues de Bordeaux, Dave Barron—San Bernardino County Sheriff's Department (Bouvier des Flandres), Frank and Sylvia Thomas—Chiheisen Akitas, Guadalupe Bravo and Katrina Cliff—Anthem American Staffordshire Terriers.

Business Owners:

Neil Glines—Elite Detail, Ed and Marcia Schlesinger—Crest Jewelers, Frank and Vicky Russo—Princess Loan Co., Chuck Berry—Imperial Auto Body, Scott Flynn—Sound Advice, Hong Shin—Charlibois Liquors, Ed Layung—Postal Annex, Jason Dahl—Jason Dahl Horse Shoeing, Patty McCoy—Pet Club, Jim Healy—Lake Mathews Video, Doug and Lisette Edmonds—Chateau Gavillan.

Special thanks to Dr. Richard W. Kobetz for writing the foreword and acting as our mentor in the security field.

CONTENTS

CONTENTS

FOREWORD

The use of animals, and dogs in particular, for protective services work is certainly not new. Dogs have served humans in this role for thousands of years, based upon the earliest drawings in caves and caverns, each dependent upon the other for mutual care and security from those who would attack, steal or threaten. This book informs the reader all about the dog as a helpmate in many ways, particularly as another security option to supplement alarms, physical security measures or nonlethal and lethal weaponry, or to stand alone as an original protective measure.

Clearly discussed is the proper selection, care, feeding and training of the animal in order to form a relationship—a bond of trust—between the dog and the handler. K-9s in security work well in particular for those who actually like dogs, not those who are afraid of them or do not respect them, or those who have had negative experiences or have cultural barriers that may block a proper relationship. Good dogs, like good owners or handlers, are difficult to cultivate. Each has a clear, distinct responsibility and the authors present the multifaceted aspects of this development.

George and Karen Duet need no endorsements concerning the proper training for dogs. Their accomplishments and credentials speak for themselves. Both authors have a genuine devotion to training that is the very essence of professionalism. What they have achieved here is something that has not been emphasized in print before, and they have shown a commitment to learning and to passing on what they have learned to others.

Good dogs and handlers are not common as this team activity is relatively new and useful literature is not extensive. This book is sure to acquire a place of honor among these texts. It is a sharply focused and clear statement on how to best serve the security needs in this area.

RICHARD W. KOBETZ, CST
Executive Director
Executive Protection Institute
Berryville, Virginia

THE BUSINESS

SECURITY K-9

INTRODUCTION

It was hot and sticky, and the jungle had the smell of dead and decaying leaves. The recent rain had left the jungles of Southeast Asia feeling like a sauna on that February morning in 1966.

I was truly uncomfortable, as were all of the other soldiers that day in the central highlands of South Vietnam. To my amazement we looked far less comfortable than the most recent arrival from Fort Benning, Georgia, Pvt. E2 Lobo, U.S. Army Scout. Lobo was an eighty-five-pound German Shepherd Dog who was still sporting a winter coat from the recent snow on the ground back home. Even so, Lobo seemed to be taking everything pretty much in stride.

The jungle trails were dotted with booby traps. The sloping hillsides held bunker complexes filled with the enemy waiting to ambush American soldiers as they walked down the trails. The dogs had been brought in to warn of the enemy's presence because of their hearing and noses. The dogs also had an uncanny ability to scent and alert on the booby traps that still carried the scent of the enemy who set them. This was a definite advantage in a place where visibility was typically less than 50 feet.

Corporal John Martin was Lobo's handler. He had always loved dogs, having grown up with a German Shepherd Dog by his side ever since he could remember. Upon joining the army and after finishing advanced infantry school, Corporal Martin had headed straight to Lackland Air Force Base in Texas to learn to be a dog handler. Now he and Lobo, after six months of working together at Fort Benning, had been sent on special assignment to Vietnam's central highlands to walk point as scouts for the army's infantry. John Martin knew how important his close relationship to Lobo had to be. One mistake could be their last. Therefore, each relied upon the other to stay alive.

John carried Lobo's food and water on his back, as well as his own. He relied on Lobo's keen senses to keep him out of booby traps and ambushes. He knew Lobo's senses literally could be the difference between life and death.

On this particularly humid February morning, we got the word to break everything down and move out to the north, right into the heart of the North Vietnamese stronghold. Everybody was tense. All weapons were double-checked. It was generally known that contact with the enemy was inevitable. The question was only who would see who first. In the jungle, the one who shoots first wins. With this in mind, Lobo and John moved forward at a deliberately slow pace down the narrow 3-foot-wide jungle trail. Lobo wore a leather tracking harness. His tracking lead stretched 15 feet behind him held by John Martin. Lobo moved slowly, one foot at a time, head thrown up in the air, ears pricked and turning from side to side like radar, his nose sniffing the air in each direction. He knew what he was sniffing for, as the odor of the Vietnamese was distinctly different from that of the Americans. The Vietnamese did not use American soap and they smelled of fish and rice, their primary diet.

The first sign of danger came no more than 100 meters from the perimeter. Lobo, who had been moving forward at a slow but steady pace, suddenly froze with one foot in the air. He resembled a bird dog pointing at game in the bushes, but his hackles were up. He stood motionless. This body language caused the hair on the nape of John Martin's neck to rise as he recognized Lobo's warning. He immediately threw his right hand up to signal to the men walking behind him to stop; the dog had alerted! Each man quickly dropped down to one knee, taking up defensive positions with weapons raised, ready to fire

John Martin crawled up to Lobo's side. "What's the matter boy?" he whispered. Lobo looked ahead and down. Following the dog's gaze, Martin saw a taut, thin wire strung across the path. It had been placed where it would catch the ankle of a walking soldier. It had been carefully concealed where the foliage grew close to the trail. Upon investigation, it was found to be attached to the D-ring of a hand grenade. If the wire had been tripped it would have caused the grenade to explode, killing or maiming whoever tripped on it and anyone else within 10 meters of the explosion.

After disarming the booby trap, the men continued to move forward, with John and Lobo walking point. After they had covered about 2 miles in nearly a three-hour period, Lobo again stopped in his tracks, hackles raised and nose in the air. This time he stretched just slightly forward as if there were an animal in the jungle ahead. He assumed a posture similar to the posture taken by a wolf stalking deer, but with one important difference; the hackles stood on his back from head to tail, showing that the intensity he displayed was for defensive reasons rather than the excitement of chasing prey.

John recognized this subtle difference. Lobo's hackles had stood before, but not to this degree. This indicated to John that the scent was much stronger and, therefore, most likely had a human source. This time when John crawled forward to try to get a fix on the subject of Lobo's attention, the dog uttered a low, guttural growl. John made the decision quickly to back off, taking Lobo back to the center of the column of men and allowing a small reconnaissance team to move forward carefully.

As the reconnaissance team moved forward, shots rang out and the team returned fire. Lobo had detected an ambush.

A battle ensued and later a perimeter was set up for the night.

Lobo's job was to replace human listening posts with his K-9 abilities. Sleeping next to his handler, any motion outside the perimeter would result in a low, guttural growl that alerted John and everyone to the presence of a probe from the enemy. During the night Lobo alerted three probes. With each alert the perimeter area was illuminated, thereby discouraging the enemy from coming any closer.

■ ■ ■

This story represents the advantages that humans and dogs have working together as a team. In Vietnam, we knew who the enemy was, but we did not always know where we would run into them. In the urban jungle, we also know there are "enemies" around, but we do not know when or where we may run across them. Business owners who choose a K-9 as a security measure allow themselves the same advantage as John Martin had with Lobo.

PREFACE

Ask the average person on the street to describe a business secu-rity K-9 and you will likely hear the following description:

> *A dog kept behind a fence. Perhaps a "junkyard dog"*
> *who's main function in life is to snarl and bare enough*
> *pearly white teeth to keep would-be burglars away.*

It is true that this could be, and sometimes is, one version of the reality of a business security K-9. However, the dog of the nineties and beyond is much more sophisticated than this junkyard image.

Currently, more and more K-9s are being utilized at every level of business as a form of security. From the small business owner who works at home, to the local convenience store, and all the way up to the corporate CEO, dogs have found a niche in the workplace. They are utilized for security along with the modern-day security system—electronic devices such as infrared detectors, security alarms, security doors, CCTVs (closed-circuit TVs) and firearms.

Today dogs are being used with modern electronic equipment, as is the case with "Rocky" the Boxer, guarding this sound recording center.

There are many reasons for the use of a security K-9, not the least of which is that on a cost-effective basis, the dog may be one of the most efficient of all security devices. It could be argued that a dog who is trained can cost the same as a security system. However, the dog is the only option that can be a physical deterrent, alarm system and bodyguard all rolled into one package. That dog is also the only option that can be utilized as a pet for pleasure as well.

So many of today's crimes are perpetrated by youth involved in gangs or drug-related violence. Many of these crimes are acts of violence upon people chosen at random, simply because they looked like an easy target. Still other crimes are planned by stalkers who observe their targets for days or weeks before striking. In either case, the business that utilizes a K-9 makes a more difficult target.

Without the added support of the personal protection specialist, the average business owner can help secure the workplace to a reasonable degree by employing many of the methods outlined in this book, the emphasis being on use of the K-9.

We sought to take the basics taught in our book, *The Home & Family Protection Dog: Selection and Training* (Howell Book House), and extend them into the more specific art of protection required of a dog in a role where the demands are greater.

Companionship and protection

CHAPTER 1

WHAT IS A
BUSINESS SECURITY K-9?

The most common use of a security dog in business is the dog who travels to and from work with the business owner. This close relationship between dog and owner dictates that the dog be incorporated into the everyday life of the owner.

The dog must get up in the morning with the owner and prepare for work, ride in a vehicle daily, interact with various people and be trained well enough to do all of this without being an added nuisance or liability.

It would not, however, be realistic to believe that you could have all of this without encountering some inconvenience. The person who considers a dog for business security must realize that there will be some changes in routine necessary to incorporate the dog into a business environment.

ADVANTAGES AND DISADVANTAGES

The person who utilizes a K-9 as an element of business security must be a dog lover. This is a necessity because the dog will be ever present in the business environment. The dog's needs, such as food, water, exercise and bathroom breaks, must be attended to. For a "dog person," this may seem to be common sense, but to a "nondog person" or novice dog owner, this may be an unreasonable expectation.

Other considerations when deciding whether or not the security K-9 is right for you are:

1. How will you transport the dog? Do you have a truck or station wagon that can be a dog carrier? Or will you use a car and devote a seat to the dog?
   Either option is potentially viable; however, without the use of an airline type (fiberglass) crate, the dog will be less safe and you will be less flexible in your ability to travel to hotels, parks and recreation areas with the dog (see Chapter VIII).

2. Is anyone working in your business environment allergic to dogs? It is not fair to someone who is expected to work in the dog's presence if they genuinely suffer from allergies.

3. Is the workplace conducive to keeping a dog? If you cannot be present with the dog because you come and go or move from site to site, this may not be a good option for you. Someone must be responsible for the dog.
   Some restrictions will be imposed by your county health department. In general, dogs are not allowed in places where food is prepared.

4. Will the dog be safe at the workplace? Special considerations may be necessary if aspects of the business are dangerous. Machine shops, welders and any environment that could be hazardous to a human would also be hazardous to the dog. This may not mean that the dog cannot be used, but precautions for its safety may be necessary.

5. Is the dog appropriate at the workplace? There are many jobs, of course, where the dog is not an option. This is true in most white-collar business environments. There is, however, an important exception to the rule. When a CEO has

been targeted for kidnapping or is being stalked for similar reasons, it may be appropriate to employ a handler-dog team.

Handler-dog teams give the advantage of the deterring presence of a K-9 without the responsibilities that go with the dog. The security specialist is responsible for the training, handling and care of the dog. The CEO in question can go about business unhindered by the presence of the K-9.

What capacities can a business security K-9 work in?

1. Shop Protection: Convenience stores, gift shops, jewelry stores, etc.
2. Mobil Business: Eighteen-wheelers, roadside repair, delivery trucks, armored vehicles, etc.
3. Personal Protection: Process servers, private investigators, repossession agents, real estate agents, etc.
4. Livestock Protection: Ranch dogs, equine investment protection, protection of cattle, sheep, etc.
5. Handler-Dog Teams: Protection of hotels, hospitals, apartment complexes, Executive and VIP security.
6. Property Protection: Area protection, vehicle protection, investment protection, etc.

As you can see, there are many potential businesses that can utilize a security K-9. The advantage of the K-9 in business security is that you have a companion and protector all rolled into one unit. Particularly for female business owners who may feel a need for an equalizer, the K-9 can be a valued companion.

Since you never know when a perpetrator is about to attack, you cannot remain armed at all times of the day, and, in fact, you would be slightly paranoid to attempt to be ready at all times. The mere presence of the dog, however, in effect makes you ready whenever the dog is with you. It gives you an extra set of eyes, and ears, and a nose as well.

The K-9 provides a high level deterrent useful in stalker or kidnap threat cases.

LIABILITIES

One of the first questions that will come to mind in the decision-making process of the business owner is liability. This is a principal concern, of course. We all want to prevent incidents that will cause injury, damage or monetary compensation. However, it is also true that as an owner, you do not have the ability to screen everyone who comes into the business for their mental soundness and likelihood of being a criminal. Because of this, we have to weigh the pros and cons of having a protection dog on the premises.

Are you more at risk by having a dog on the premises or by not having one? There are many factors weighed into this decision, not the least of which is the mental balance of the dog as well as the training that both dog and handler have received. We would caution the potential owner of the business security K-9 *not to attempt this without professional assistance.* This is because the average person is likely to overestimate or underestimate the dog's propensity to become aggressive. Either of these can get you into trouble. For example:

> *Suppose a person took an untrained German Shepherd Dog to work on a regular basis. From time to time the dog alerted and showed defensive behavior toward people the dog perceived to be different or a threat of some sort. It may follow that the owner would have a false sense of security and believe that this dog would protect when the need arose. When the need did arise, if the dog did not come to the owner's aid and did not recognize the threat or only stood and barked while the owner was in a physical confrontation with an assailant, it would then be too late to teach the dog how to respond properly. This is an important reason why a dog should be professionally trained. It will increase the odds of proper response by 80 to 90 percent.*

On the other hand:

> *If the business owner had a dog, whether trained or untrained, who was very dominant and aggressive by nature, and the owner was not trained to handle the dog, that untrained owner might not properly perceive what the dog would regard as a threat. Therefore, if a person made a move such as swinging a baseball bat or a crutch near the owner, this could trigger an unwarranted aggressive response from the dog. The owner would not be prepared for this. More importantly, the owner would not have the foresight to perceive the danger and either remove it from the dog's presence or calm the dog with a command.*

As you can see with either of these examples, the education of both owner and dog is very important.

LEGALITIES

Legally, you are responsible for your dog's behavior. It is important that you are cognizant of your dog's behavior and the animal's likely reactions to various stimuli. If you have no desire to take on this responsibility, then this particular security option is not right for you.

Legally, you are obligated to advise your patrons of the dog's presence. You can do this by posting a sign that should not scare your patrons away, but should work as a deterrent to criminals. The sign should be a combination of obvious colors, and should be large enough to be noticeable. It is a good idea to have the head of a dog on the sign to ensure that even those who may not be able to read the sign can recognize its meaning. You do not want to condemn the dog, by putting up signs that could be used against you in a court situation, like "Trespassers Will Be Eaten" or "Warning! Bad Dog." Rather, "Warning! Dog on Premises" is sufficient.

Accidents can happen without warning! To avoid them, take care not to let the problem arise!

A dog who functions as a store mascot must be very tolerant. Shown are "Nero" and friends in "Easter wear."

You should check with your state or local municipality to be sure about the laws that pertain to your area, as every country, state and county can differ regarding regulations about dogs. Some areas also specify the color, type and size of the sign that is to be posted.

Anywhere you go, you are expected to protect your dog as well as protect others from your dog. Whether or not you are legally required to do the following, these are some things you should plan on for the safety of the dog and others:

1. Post signs at all etrances to your business or residence as to the presence of your dog (an added deterrent to crime).
2. Keep a leash and collar on your dog whenever off your property, i.e., from your business to your vehicle, etc.
3. Transport the dog safely using a pet carrier or safety harness in case of an accident.
4. Carry water and water bowl for your dog. **Never** leave the dog in a hot vehicle.
5. Do not let people constantly interact with the dog (unless the dog is a mascot). If a dog is trained for protection, this will only undermine the training and increase your liability.
6. Rabies shots must remain current on a protection dog, or any dog for that matter. This is especially true for a dog who spends much of the time in public. Other inoculations that should be current for the sake of the dog's health are DHLP, parvovirus, coronavirus, and possible Lyme disease or any other local contagious disease.

COMPANIONSHIP AND PROTECTION

One of the main attractions of a business security K-9 is the companionship aspect. To a dog lover, the idea of having a dog along all the time is a positive rather than a negative. It is very much like the old adage of the cup being half empty or half full. It depends upon your perception.

One client of ours who has a Bouvier des Flandres in a pet store reported that her business increased markedly when Nero became the store mascot. Nero dresses in different costumes for various holidays. He wears a red, white and blue top hat for the Fourth of July, a Santa Claus hat for Christmas and in the summer you can catch him wearing a tank top, sun visor and sunglasses. All of the kids who frequent the shopping center stop by to say hello to Nero. They often bring their parents along with them. This, of course, is good for business. Although Nero has never been *protection* trained, he was raised by trainers from eight weeks of age. He was Obedience trained and conditioned to be courageous. As a mascot, he is expected to be social, but his size and demeanor also help to keep the "bad guys" away.

Because the business security K-9 is constantly by your side, you are relatively well covered by a bodyguard at all times. Since you never know where you might be assaulted (i.e., in the street, at your car or in your place of business) your odds of being accosted are greatly reduced with the constant presence of your dog. This is a real attraction particularly to anyone who often works alone or works late hours, weekends or holidays.

YOUR THREAT ASSESSMENT

It is wise for everyone, with today's atmosphere of ever-increasing violence, to conduct his or her own "threat assessment."

A threat assessment is done by considering several facts about the environment that we live and work in. Necessary facts with regard to area crime rates, community attitudes, local economics, gang problems, drug traffic, as well as individual grudges or social attitudes that may be prevalent in a community, should be taken into consideration.

In order to make an educated threat assessment, you may want to do some research at the local library or police station, or in the local newspaper. If you have lived or worked in the area for any length of time, you may already have a very good feel for the crime in your area. You or a neighbor or local business owner may have already been victimized. In any case, you will find it beneficial to take a pen and paper and begin to follow the steps to conduct a threat assessment.

WHY DO I NEED TO CONDUCT A THREAT ASSESSMENT?

We conduct a threat assessment because it is impossible to choose the proper level of protection or amount of protection necessary if we do not understand the risk we are facing. Once the potential risks are recognized and evaluated, a determination as to the appropriate type and amount of protection options will be necessary to control those risks.

As you determine where your risks are highest, remember that it is wisest to *avoid risk* whenever possible. Therefore, if you can drive around a bad part of town rather than through it, this would be wise. Likewise, if you were to discover that the area you plan to locate in has a history of hate crimes toward your race, religion or gender, you may want to rethink moving your business there. There are many circumstances where, because of the economics or deterioration of an area, business owners may find themselves facing risks they have never had to face before.

When avoidance is not possible, it is then necessary to minimize the consequences of risk. To do this, you must realize what potential risk exists and the consequences of that risk. As the same time, realize what the consequences of ignoring the risk would be.

Next, you will need to realize that security by its very nature creates some inconvenience. The inconvenience may be as minor as the need to install an extra deadbolt, to the greater inconvenience that certain executives and VIPs incur when employing protective agents who stay with them wherever they go. A good risk assessment must take into consideration *both risk and convenience:* for as more protective measures are taken, there is more inconvenience.

Nobody is completely without risk. People who live in "good neighborhoods" are victimized regularly. We cannot restrict our movement and associations with people to minimize our risk because we would cease to be effective in business if we did this.

Now, with pen and paper ready, go through the following steps, making notes to yourself as to your own threat assessment. If necessary, gather facts and statistics before you proceed.

STEP # 1 DEFINE YOUR RISK

What are the most likely risks that you will encounter? Robbery, assault, rape, murder, mugging, street crime, gang violence, carjacking, equipment theft, kidnapping, terrorism, vandalism, malicious mischief, hate crimes, verbal assaults, antagonism and so on.

Define the problem as thoroughly as possible for yourself, taking care not to focus on the area as the problem, but rather on the problem itself, such as drug traffic or gang violence.

Next, you need to identify where the risks are likely to occur: at home, leaving your home, in the car on the way to work, entering the workplace, at the workplace, during your movements to see clients, visits to warehouses or docks, closing the store, on the way to the bank, working late, on your way home, and so on.

Again, define the problem as clearly as possible and who is the problem.

STEP # 2 IDENTIFY YOUR SECURITY OPTIONS

There are five options you can choose from. In many cases, you may be able to implement options at times from all five categories. Although this text is primarily addressing the business security K-9, it is our belief that the more options (within reason) you implement, the more secure you will be as you make yourself a much more difficult target.

Your options are as follows:

1. Avoid
2. Escape
3. Deter
4. Detect
5. Defend

Avoid

As previously stated, if you can avoid trouble without unreasonable inconvenience, it would be wise to do so. Why put yourself or your loved ones in danger if you have a choice? If you can choose to do business elsewhere, drive a different route or change merchandise so as not to attract a certain type of person to your store, this may be one option for you.

It is always better to avoid confrontation if possible.

Escape

It is always better to escape danger than to face it. Think about it. What purpose is served facing danger unless it is necessary to save another person? There is no object or amount of merchandise worth risking your life over.

If you see gang members carrying automatic weapons entering your store, are you wiser to escape through a back door or into a safe room? Are you going to argue with them over a few hundred dollars and a case of beer? A safe room is a room that has been reinforced specifically for security purposes. Imagine that you don't have a rear exit, or that it is blocked. The safe room should be a place that you can retreat for a last stand. A bathroom is a good safe room. It already has a supply of water. You must reinforce the walls and the door. You will want to make sure that the door cannot be kicked or bypassed easily. A reinforced window that can only be opened from the inside is a good idea. Have a cellular telephone or at least a cordless with direct dial to the police, or have an additional monitored security system that you can rely on as well. A backup power source should be considered, as an alarm system will fail if the power source is cut off. What you are attempting to do is escape, call the police and defend yourself if necessary. To defend yourself you have the options of a security K-9 and a weapon.

We all hope that we will never be victims. Unfortunately, any security-related professional will tell you that too many people don't implement a security plan until *after* they become victims.

This is like trying to shut the barn door after the horse is out. It's too late! It is much wiser to ask yourself ahead of time, "How will I deter, detect and defend against crime?"

Deter

Our *first objective* is to deter crime so that when it comes along it decides to keep going. How do we do that? We can visually make the business look difficult to assault because it appears to be owned by a security-conscious person. It has security bars, signs in the windows that warn of alarms and security K-9s, maybe a closed-circuit TV and a two-way mirror so the potential criminal doesn't know who might be watching. For outside areas, alarm systems that make noise and illuminate the area are a plus.

K-9 security—in the form of one or two dogs with the proper size, temperament and training—is one of the best deterrents, especially when humans are present, such as the owner or a handler-dog team. *A dog adds two problems to a criminal's difficulty: vocal warning and unpredictability.*

Random crime is less likely to happen, as the juvenile who decides to assault the store owner over the counter is less likely to do so if there is a dog visible behind the counter.

Detect

In order to be able to escape or defend yourself, you need to detect the presence of the perpetrator.

Security systems that utilize electronics, such as motion detectors, infrared sensors, detector cells, have their rightful place, but for the most part they are not designed for use during business hours when people normally come and go. *By the time an alarm is triggered during business hours, the business has already encountered the criminal.*

The security K-9 has hearing at least ten times greater than humans. The K-9's nose is the greatest asset, scenting a minimum of one hundred times more acutely than humans. With these two

K-9 abilities, business people—whether in the store, office, vehicle or street—have much greater ability to detect a person hiding in the shadows or acting suspicious in a store.

When speaking of purely the detection aspect of the K-9, the dog can be any size. The most important asset for detection is awareness.

Defend

In the defense aspect of security, there are just a few options. Your choices: self-defense by means of martial arts, pepper spray, mace, stun gun, firearms, personal protection agent (if money is no object) or handler-dog team working together.

The security K-9 can work as a team with the business owner. The team can work like a police K-9 and handler would. The dog gives the human precious time to react and defend himself/herself, typically with a firearm.

You will note that in the areas of deterrence, detection and defense, *a dog is the only option that can do all three.* There is one exception: a human security agent or agent with a K-9. This option is expensive and usually reserved for VIPs; however, it is becoming common for large businesses such as hospitals, hotels and corporations to request security K-9 teams. It is also becoming more common for communities or shopping centers to band together and hire such teams.

STEP 3: EVALUATING AND SELECTING YOUR OPTIONS

Now you must look at your options based on things such as cost, life-style, what or who you are attempting to protect and so on.

For instance, if you work in a high-rise office building from nine to five and jet-set around the country, there is probably little use for a K-9 in your life, unless you have a serious threat and hire protective services that include a handler-dog team. However, if you do not have the means to afford a handler-dog team, but have a threat and own a small store or drive an eighteen-wheeler, you may choose to own a security K-9.

As with other options, cost, life-style and mobility of the security options all have to be considered, chosen and implemented.

STEP 4: EVALUATING THE RESULTS AND MAKING ADJUSTMENTS

Your final step after implementing security options is to evaluate how comfortable you are with the options you have chosen and how well they are working. One of the biggest problems with evaluating the effectiveness of your security is that if it works, *nothing happens.* Your success can be based on *nothing happening.*

One family who chose K-9s as a security measure said, "We can only report that before the dogs, we were held at gunpoint three times in a three-month period. After the dogs were in, we have not been held up again in seven years."

With regard to adjustments, you need to adjust your security measures if the environment changes, the measures chosen are not effective for the situation or the threat evaluation was not assessed properly.

A good example of a business owner who did not assess his own threat well was a car repossession agent who, after several confrontations with people, decided he wanted a K-9. The dog would ride along with him and act as the agent's ears and eyes to warn of someone coming and to act as a deterrent. Faced with the decision to buy one of two Dobermans, he chose the less expensive of the two, who was sold as an alarm and deterrent, not an apprehension dog. It cost one-half of what the other dog cost. In a matter of weeks, the agent reported that the dog had successfully deterred several individuals and groups of people from accosting him. One night, the agent ran across a 6-foot 4-inch, 270-pound man on drugs who was not deterred by the dog and proceeded to "knock the dog upside the head" and pulverize the repo agent. The agent had to rethink his threat assessment and later returned to purchase the apprehension dog.

IS A SECURITY K-9 RIGHT FOR YOU?

We are not suggesting, by any means, that the protection K-9 used in business is for everyone. It certainly is not right for many people, particularly those who do not own the business in question.

The following are examples of people who might find the use of a K-9 for business or personal protection to be an advantage:

1. Anyone who owns a small retail store and often works alone or with a small number of employees.
2. Dog lovers who wish to incorporate the dog as a mascot/ deterrent for the store or business.
3. People in a particular high-risk profession, i.e., process servers, private investigators, repossessing agents, etc.
4. CEOs, attorneys or any head of an organization who may be targeted by a stalker. In some situations the dog may only be able to be utilized at home unless a handler-dog team is hired. This may be necessary in a high-risk situation. A dog who protects a CEO at home can also be considered a business security K-9, because the dog is protecting the organization's chief executive officer.
5. People who enjoy the companionship of dogs and who enjoy being able to break the ice with other people by using the dog as a focal point for conversation. Dogs are great conversation pieces. Many of our single clients can attest to this fact.
6. Men or women who, because of the nature of their business, have to carry cash, jewelry or important documents to and from their place of business.
7. People who must work in darkness on a late shift when there is more chance of criminal activities. People who must travel in a vehicle at night, such as couriers, eighteen-wheel-truck drivers, workers who frequent docks or warehouses where they are alone in a strange place in darkness.

These people should *not* consider a security K-9:

1. People who are allergic to dogs or who have employees that are allergic to dogs.
2. People who are not physically capable of controlling a large, active protection dog.
3. People who don't like dogs or the responsibilities that go along with them.
4. People who will not be responsible enough to be a dog handler and be with the dog at all times or to leave that dog with a responsible party.
5. People who want to use the dog for illegal purposes, such as guarding drugs or stolen property, or who do not provide a safe environment by having the dog in an illegal situation.
6. People who, by the nature of their business, do not have a predictable schedule and may find themselves in a situation where a dog is not appropriate.

Dogs can adapt to many different working environments. Shown is "Beau," with owner Jason Dahl, a farrier.

CHAPTER II

JOB DESCRIPTIONS

There are four categories in which the business security K-9 may be classified. Among these are several subcategories that serve as examples of why the stereotypical image of the dog-behind-a-fence as a business security K-9 is antiquated.

The categories are:

1. **Shop Protection Dogs.** Use: Business and personal protection for the business owner. Examples: Convenience stores jewelry stores, gas stations, gift shops, florists, etc.
2. **Dual Purpose Dogs.** Use: Mascots for business as well as alarm/deterrent dogs. Examples: Ranch dogs, store mascots, watch dogs on yachts, or a dog who accompanies the owner in whatever activity the owner is involved in and can double as protection for the owner at the same time.
3. **Property Protection Dogs.** Use: To protect an area, a vehicle, equipment, business assets, etc. Examples: Dogs who protect eighteen-wheelers, heavy equipment, livestock, car lots, money or a briefcase, etc.
4. **Handler–K-9 Teams.** Use: To patrol with a handler and protect a person, place or thing from danger. Examples:

The presence of a K-9 in a store is a deterrent to crime.

A mascot can be a large or small friendly companion who can also serve as an alarm/deterrent.

Handler-dog teams who patrol estates, hospitals, hotels, apartment complexes or VIPs who are in need of protection.

It is very important that the owner has the *entire* job description in mind when choosing the dog. This is advisable because the proper temperament is crucial to the success of your project. This is discussed further in Chapter IV, The Right K-9 Temperament for Your Needs.

SHOP PROTECTION K-9s—BUSINESS AND PERSONAL PROTECTION

This is the most common business security K-9. This dog accompanies the owner to the store and home again in the evening. The dog's primary responsibility is to protect the owner from harm. Although the dog is fully capable of protecting the merchandise in the store, this is not the primary function. The dog's *primary* function is that of a bodyguard. This dog needs to be trained in protection Levels I through III as well as in: defense of the handler (moving and stationary), vehicle protection, building search and motionless threat.

Teaching the dog to walk backward in the Heel position—in order to defend behind the handler or to simply turn to watch behind the handler, for example, at an ATM—is an excellent talent for the dog who's major function is person protection.

DUAL PURPOSE K-9s—LARGE OR SMALL BREEDS USED AS ALARM/DETERRENTS

This is one job description where small breeds can be used as well as large breeds. Any dog who is aware enough to keep an eye on strangers, and sound an alarm in the event that something seems wrong, can be an alarm dog. To be a physical deterrent as well, the dog must be of substantial size. Even if the dog is not trained in apprehension work, the size and demeanor of the dog can be an excellent deterrent.

■ ■ ■

A good example of a dog used as a mascot/deterrent is Nero, the ninety-pound Bouvier des Flandres previously mentioned, who works as a mascot for The Pet Club in Riverside, California. Even though he looks quite the clown in costume, Nero commands respect from the patrons of the store. He frequently growls a warning after-hours when he detects a person in the shadows of the dimly lit parking lot as his owner walks to her car.

Another type of mascot is Sabbath, a Labrador Retriever who works at Kidsville Daycare. Sabbath loves the children and keeps an eye on the comings and goings of adults. Sabbath recognizes the parents and announces their comings and goings, but reserves an entirely different type of bark for strangers and delivery people. Sabbath makes it his responsibility to let those delivery people know they should just leave their packages and go!

■ ■ ■

A small dog can be just as efficient an alarm as a large dog. As everyone knows, a small dog can make a big fuss vocally. If a small dog is used for detection and alarm, the business owner should then have a plan that does *not* rely upon the little dog to deter and defend against crime.

Another example of a dual purpose K-9 is the ranch dog. A dog employed by a ranch may have several duties. This dog may herd cattle or sheep, ride along in a vehicle when moving livestock, guard the trailers while the owner is away or guard the barns where the prize horses are kept. Many ranch dogs serve as vocal alarms, announcing the arrival of visitors. For the serious work of protecting livestock that represents a large investment to the owner, the more serious and aggressive property protection dog may be used around the perimeter of the barn or the area being protected.

PROPERTY PROTECTION K-9s—YARD, VEHICLE AND INVESTMENT PROTECTION

There are two different types of property protection K-9s:

1. The antisocial "fence" dog who is simply put inside a perimeter in order to keep people out.
2. The personal protection dog who is also taught to guard objects. The object may be as small as a briefcase or as large as a horse trailer or vehicle.

THE FENCE DOG

Dogs who are too aggressive to live in a home environment and may otherwise have to be destroyed are good candidates for fence dogs. The best fence dogs are *antisocial.* There are many factors that can make a dog antisocial:

1. The dog may be an "alpha" personality by nature—a ten on the temperament scale (see Chapter IV). This means the dog is very aggressive but lacks respect for handler, which means there is no "off" switch on the dog. At best, a person can be *accepted* by the dog, but the dog will *never* take a *subservient* position to anyone.
2. The dog may be genetically unbalanced. A dog too aggressive because of poor breeding may not be consistently an alpha dog, but also may not be balanced enough to trust in a home environment.

A highly trained protection dog, exceptionally high in Defense Drive, will make a very good fence dog. The drawback to this dog is cost. This dog is highly effective in many job descriptions and will bring top dollar. A fence dog is put in the position of a "throwaway." By using this dog, you are accepting the possibility that the dog may be killed by a gun, crossbow, poison or other means, or the dog may be let out if a fence is cut or if someone can manage to open a gate and create a diversion.

"Sabbath" at work at Kidsville Daycare.

The fence dog should be naturally antisocial in order to keep people away without the assistance of a human handler.

We least like to deal with this aspect of K-9 security because we feel that the dog is at a real disadvantage in 90 percent of all cases. The major reason is that in this work the dog is expected to work alone. When you consider this, you must remember that dogs do not have reasoning ability. This means that a human who wishes to steal something from a property guarded by a fence dog has time to reason how to get past the dog. The person may try to sweet-talk or bribe the dog. This is why the dog needs to be antisocial. If this doesn't work, would-be thieves may revert to poison or any number of other methods.

The best situation for a fence dog is behind a wrought-iron fence or block wall. This makes the fence much harder to penetrate and gives the dog an added advantage. When possible, having an inner perimeter fence is very effective. This solves the fence cutting problem and keeps people from coming into direct contact with the dogs unless they penetrate the first perimeter fence. If motion detectors can be used between the two perimeter fences, it will be much harder for the thief to penetrate unnoticed to the enclosure with the dog (see diagram). This also keeps enough distance between the thief and the dog to ensure that the dog threatens vocally, as dogs tend to bark more when the thief is at a distance. Infrared sensors can be used inside of buildings for added security, if desired. Dogs outside the buildings won't set the sensors off.

K-9s should be considered simply as one weapon in the security arsenal. They should not be considered as an end-all to security, much the same as any option from alarm systems to weapons—the more layers of coverage you have, the better off you are.

The Fence Dog Handler

There should always be a minimum of two people who have a relationship with the fence dog. You may choose a main handler and an alternate. There are many reasons for at least two people. Employees come and go, and in case a handler leaves the business, there must be an alternate with whom the dog is familiar. People

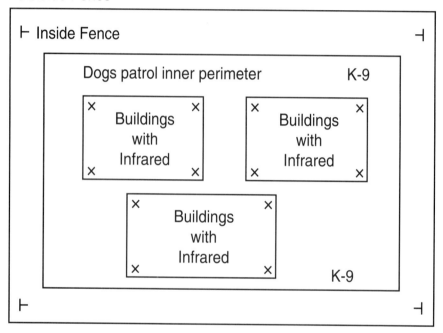

Outside Fence

Inside Fence

Dogs patrol inner perimeter K-9

Buildings with Infrared

Buildings with Infrared

Buildings with Infrared

K-9

× = Infrared
K-9 = Dogs
⊢ = Motion detectors

Dogs who have direct access to the fence line are easier to bypass than those who work behind an inner fence.

also get sick or take vacations. Dogs have to be fed, given fresh water, cleaned up after and maintained 365 days of the year.

The fence dog handler does not need as much schooling as the handler who will handle a dog in public. However, training for the handler is still important because there may be times when the dog has someone cornered in the fenced area. The dog must have enough of a relationship with the handler to listen to commands. The fence dog's obedience does not have to be exact, and it can be motivated by food rewards, but the dog *must understand* and *respond to commands*. The easiest way to make friends with a naturally antisocial dog is with food or a toy. The fence dog owner should spend the first three weeks playing with, feeding and getting to know the dog. If you are going to use a toy or ball to get to know the dog, there should not be any demands on the dog to drop the ball or toy. It is much wiser to use several balls and alternate toys to keep the dog's attention.

The fence dog must also accept a muzzle when being taken to the veterinarian. This is another reason the dog must have a relationship with a handler. You cannot expect an antisocial dog to stand passively while being thoroughly poked and probed by a complete stranger.

The Fence Dog During Business Hours

The fence dog must be kept away from the public and any employees of the company not directly involved with the handling, care and maintenance of the dog. This means that a fence dog must have a dog run that is isolated away from business activities and must be equipped with basic food, fresh water, shade and shelter from the elements.

One major problem in keeping security dogs in runs all day is their constant alerting and barking at employees or clientele. This is another reason for the use of crates or the necessity of having the dog run in an out-of-the-way location.

Crates can also be utilized in an out-of-the-way location in an office. This allows the dogs to be kept inside in air conditioning

A dog who is entrusted with guarding an object must be intelligent and well-trained. Shown is Ch. Kingsden's Firestorm Dallas, guarding a rare motorcycle.

during the day in hot climates or out of rain or snow in cold climates. Since the dogs are outside all night running a perimeter, crates allow them a typical eight-hour rest period during the day, ensuring they rest so that they are wakeful and active at night.

Letting the dogs come into direct contact with people can only undermine their working ability either by oversocialization, which brings down the dog's Defense Drive, or by constant agitation without the object of their aggressive behavior reacting to the dog's aggression. Therefore, *the fence dog should never be allowed to socialize with anyone other than the designated handlers.*

DOGS WHO GUARD OBJECTS

This dog is altogether a different creature from the antisocial fence dog. They are as different as night and day.

The dog entrusted with guarding an object must be highly intelligent. This is advanced protection work at its highest level. The best parallel we can draw is the difference between the barroom bouncer, who relies on appearance and muscle to intimidate, and the executive protection specialist, who wears a coat and tie and uses mental prowess and training to protect the client. The fence dog is much like the bouncer using appearance and demeanor as tools to control the environment. A dog taught to guard a briefcase, for instance, must use mental skills and be watchful. At the same time, if a person brushes up against the dog or shakes hands with the handler, the dog should remain calm and unruffled.

There are two methods of guarding an object that a dog may be expected to learn. The first we consider to be basic.

Guarding a Car

Guarding a car can be taught to any dog with enough defense drive. This type of defense is primarily of cosmetic value. As you can imagine, no one in their right mind will try to get into a car with a snarling dog inside.

The owner must be cognizant of the potential destruction that a dog is capable of rendering when guarding a car. It is true that the more effort you put into training, the less likely a dog will decide to "trash" your car while you're away. A lot depends on the individual dog. Some dogs by nature are high-strung and take out frustration by mouthing things. Others are gentler. It depends on the specific dog, but, in general, you may have better luck with a Bouvier des Flandres, a Giant Schnauzer or an Australian Cattle Dog than you would with a Bullmastiff or Dogue de Bordeaux. If you remember the movie *Turner & Hooch,* the destruction that Hooch did to Turner's car is more likely if the wrong dog is used for vehicle protection.

If the dog is to be used in a vehicle for trips to the city, bank runs, repossessions or process serving, for example, there are some helpful electronic devices on the market that can signal a dog for help, lower a window or open a door automatically so that the K-9 can come to your rescue (see Chapter III). When this is the desired avenue, the dog must be taught how to respond from the vehicle.

Common uses of dogs to protect vehicles are as follows:

1. To ride "shotgun" in eighteen-wheelers.
2. To protect horses or livestock on ranches or in transit.
3. To protect their owners' tools or supplies (construction workers, landscape trucks, armor trucks, plumbers, electricians, etc.).
4. To protect the business owner or CEO in the vehicle from car jacking, kidnapping, car theft, etc.

Caution: An enclosed vehicle, making it impossible for a dog to have access to someone in order to bite, is very safe. In a truck, a shell can be utilized. A dog should *never* guard an object without a human handler nearby unless the area is secured from the public and warning signs are posted.

Guarding an Object Using a Handler-Dog Team

The most highly trained dogs can be taught to guard an object, such as a briefcase, on command. The handler simply touches whatever is to be guarded and gives the dog the command. The dog

A dog can be taught to guard a briefcase or any valuable object. Anyone approaching is safe **unless they attempt to take the object.**

Steve Scheratis of Security Force Unlimited with his K-9 "Cezan." This team is used to clear particularly dangerous gang properties.

then knows, through training, to bite anyone, other than the handler, who tries to touch the object. At the handler's command, the dog will also cease to guard the object.

While under this command, the dog knows to be watchful of anyone who comes close. However, the dog also understands that someone brushing against it, stepping on its tail or pounding a fist on a table is not a provoker—unless the person reaches for the object.

For someone who is carrying a large sum of money or important documents, this dog may be added benefit to the security team (for further information, see page 35 on "The Use of K-9s in Executive Security").

Guarding a Child

A dog can be taught to guard a person as well as an object. In other words, as the handler, I can make myself or a member of my family—for instance, my child—the object to guard. This is something you might use only in an extreme emergency, such as a kidnap case. If the object is the child, then the dog will not allow anyone to touch that child. Once you teach the dog the rules, the object could be almost anything.

HANDLER–K-9 TEAMS—SECURITY PATROL, EXECUTIVE AND VIP PROTECTION

Without a doubt, the best way to use a K-9 is a handler-dog team. In most small business situations the owner becomes the handler in the handler-dog team. Other businesses prefer to make an employee the handler. And yet, others (on the upper end financially) will hire specialists to do the work for them.

K-9 SECURITY PATROL

Many security companies have now added K-9 security patrol as an option to their clients. This is especially true of the apartment complexes that the government subsidizes for low-income housing. There tends to be a lot of gang activity, drug traffic and violence in these areas.

The dogs are used only for deterrent purposes and for protection of the handlers. They are not ever taken off the leash and they do not have the authority to apprehend a fleeing suspect. They are allowed to defend their handlers and they are very effective at dispersing crowds.

One such security team—Steve Trachta and Steve Scheratis of Security Force Unlimited—reports that when they step onto a property *without* the K-9s, they are verbally harassed and threatened regularly. When they show up *with* their K-9s in tow, everyone just "magically" disappears.

HOSPITAL AND HOTEL SECURITY K-9s

Hospitals and hotels in large cities that are plagued with urban violence have begun using handler-dog teams. Many hospitals now have handler-dog teams in the emergency rooms. Urban violence used to stop at the doorsteps of these hospitals. It used to be that the hospital was somewhat of a "no fire zone." It was an unwritten law that the hospital was one place you didn't shoot your enemy. Unfortunately, this is not necessarily the case anymore. The doctors themselves have requested the use of the K-9s in order to protect themselves and their patients. The K-9 is used mainly as a deterrent, but is on call when necessary to actually serve as a buffer from violence for the doctors in the emergency rooms.

HOTEL SECURITY

In some of the smaller hotels and motels, the owner is part of the handler-dog team. In larger hotels, the handler-dog team forms part of the hotel security force. The teams may work on a regular basis or just be on call in case of violence or civil unrest, as during the 1992 Los Angeles riots.

The Black Tie K-9 is totally controlled by voice, is unob-
trusive and a pleasure to have around, even in the most
formal settings.

When the executive or VIP utilizes K-9s with Personal Protection Specialists,
it allows the VIP to be free of all responsibilities associated with the use
of dogs.

TRAINING OF K-9 SECURITY HANDLER-DOG TEAMS

In order to be effective, K-9 security teams must spend many hours in training. The handler and dog must share a bond, as each relies on the other in case they must go into action. The team must have practiced the "3Ds" of security dog training: deter, detect and defend. This amounts to many hours practicing moves and defensive scenarios. The security K-9 team is much like a police K-9 unit, except they are not allowed to pursue a fleeing suspect. They are allowed to apprehend and detain a suspect for the police.

The K-9's use as a deterrent is probably its primary asset. A human's *fear* of being bitten by a dog comes into play when a K-9 is employed. If you talk to some troublemakers, you will hear that they think nothing of harassing an armed security agent or officer because they know that the agent is bound by the law and is restricted from using a firearm. They are more worried about the handler with the K-9 who hasn't read the law and they know they cannot as easily predict how the dog may react.

THE USE OF K-9S IN EXECUTIVE SECURITY

A Personal Protection Specialist is a person who is trained in the art of providing protection for his/her principal (employer). This service is not inexpensive and, therefore, is utilized mainly by celebrities, political figures, religious leaders, corporate CEOs and other VIPs.

The Personal Protection Specialist's role, recently dramatized in the movie *The Bodyguard,* has until recently been a relatively unknown field. For general understanding, the Personal Protection Specialist's duties are on par with the duties of Secret Service Agents. In a nutshell, the Personal Protection Specialist assumes the responsibilities of providing protection in an appropriate manner, using a variety of "tools." Getting the principal to appointments on time, providing for the comfort of the principal and preventing incidents that may cause harm or embarrassment are all duties of the Personal Protection Specialist.

The K-9 that is used in executive security should have a temperament consistent with the role to be played in the protection of the principal. For instance, if the dog is to be used for patrol purposes only, the dog may have a temperament that is on par with a police K-9. The patrol dog will never come in contact with the principal or guests on the property, and therefore, it is not necessary for this K-9 to be refined where manners are concerned.

On the other hand, if the K-9 is expected to remain quietly in the principal's residence or vehicle (which may be the case in a high-risk scenario or a stalker case), this dog must be what we call a "black tie" K-9.

The Black Tie K-9

Most people think of the security K-9 as a snarly mouth full of teeth waiting to attack. While this may be true of the antisocial fence dog, there is no place for the antisocial dog in executive protection.

The black tie K-9 (as the title reflects) is genteel. This dog is calm, well mannered and *totally voice controlled.* It takes a very special dog to be a black tie K-9. This dog is typically three to five years of age, is very social by nature, but very effective when called into action. The black tie K-9 is perfectly balanced in temperament, with 50 percent defense and 50 percent prey drives.

The K-9 utilized in the principal's residence must be calm and well mannered. This dog must not be excessively vocal by nature and should not whine or fidget. This dog should be very social with people, not overly defensive and totally voice controlled. The Rottweiler is a good choice for this role. This is a breed of the Mastiff type and therefore comfortable on a Down/Stay for extended periods. On the other hand, the patrol dog generally needs to be leaner and more active and possess greater endurance. The German Shepherd Dog or Belgian Malinois would be more suitable for this type or work.

When the principal is a dog lover and personally owns dogs, protection using K-9s is much easier and more effective.

When K-9s are posted at entrances, they are excellent visual deterrents and invited guests feel more secure.

ESTATE SECURITY

The first, and most likely, use for the security K-9 is in estate protection. In order to be highly visible, dogs can be posted at gates and entrances. They also can be used to patrol with an agent at set intervals. In either case, K-9s are an excellent visual deterrent, the dog aids the handler in remaining awake and alert, especially at night. The K-9's keen hearing and sense of smell are excellent aids to the agent in darkness. The dog tends to boost the morale of the agents, adding an element of friendship to both the handler and the team. The K-9 and handler checking the alertness of the posted agents in the early morning hours is a good way to keep the agents awake and alert.

In addition to fixed posts or roving patrols for particularly high-risk situations, the K-9 can be used in close proximity to the principal. A good example of a high-risk VIP protection scenario would be when the deposed and exiled Shah of Iran came to the United States as Dr. Richard W. Kobetz explains: "The Iranians had put out a death notice on him saying anyone responsible for his death would sit at the right hand of Allah. This represents the heaviest possible of threats."

In a case such as this, you may use explosives detection K-9s and multiple handler-dog teams both inside and outside of the estate, as well as other agents and security measures. In some cases, the explosives detection dog is the highest priority. This was the case when a bomb was left in an executive washroom. The intended victim was not hurt; however, another bomb was then thrown in this person's backyard. Luckily, the bomb rolled into the swimming pool. When security was arranged for in this situation, an explosives detection K-9 was an essential tool.

ADVANCE WORK

The K-9 is also of use in advance work. Advance work is the process of checking in advance on the security of the area where the principal is due to arrive, as well as preparing the accommodations and making sure that everything is in working order. Explosives detection K-9s are a valuable addition to an advance if the principal is assessed as a high risk or he/she is to speak in public or to attend functions that have been announced in the media. The K-9's exceptional sense of smell cuts the time needed to clear an area to a minimum. The Labrador Retriever is excellent performing this type of work.

MOVEMENT

Movement brings up another potential opportunity for the use of a K-9, which can be brought along in a follow car when desired. Automatic remote control door and window openers are available if the K-9 is not to be outside of the vehicle unless needed. When utilizing the K-9, vehicles of choice would be enclosed trucks, four-by-fours, station wagons or vans. If a car is used, K-9 enclosures may be purchased for long-term use. One country utilizes a limousine that is specially fitted with a K-9 compartment in the trunk area, where the dog rests out of the way, unless called into action.

Movement with a K-9 can look as low profile as a stroll in the park with a dog, or as complex as the use of dogs to perform a diamond pattern or crowd control line to keep people from crowding the principal. In order to prevent accidental bites in crowd situations, a muzzle can be worn with a quick-release drawstring designed to release only when the handler deems necessary. A muzzle is worn in a crowd situation because people may try to reach out and pet the dog or pull its tail or ears.

LANDING ZONES

Landing zones—or any area that needs to be secured for the comings and goings of the principal—are another area of possible use for the K-9. Handler-dog teams can fan out in either a diamond or pyramid formation (see diagrams). Formations are determined by the area size, terrain, strength or the team and threat assessment.

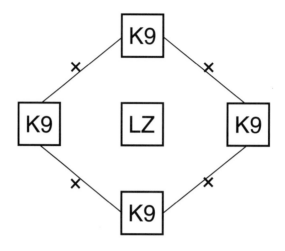

DIAMOND FORMATION

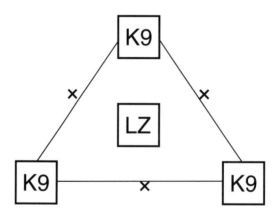

PYRAMID FORMATION

The diamond and pyramid formations can be used in various situations. In this example, LZ is used to indicate a landing zone. On very tight jobs (high-threat level), one of these formations may be utilized.

Formations would also be determined by the mode of transportation, such as private aircraft or helicopter, and whether or not the airstrip is private or there are other aircraft operating in the area. (*x* = agents, *K-9* = handler-dog team.)

K-9s Used in Stalker Cases

An excellent situation for a K-9 is a stalker case. An agent in the residence in the evening can be a little intrusive. The K-9, however, can be at the principal's side regardless of the room the person is in.

Cost is another factor. The K-9 costs less than an agent, especially for a long-term protective assignment. The principal purchases the dog and is given basic handling instructions. At the end of the assignment, there is the option of keeping the dog or turning it back to the trainer.

K-9s are very *visual and high profile.* This high visibility allows them to be used as deterrents or diversions. A stalker may determine that the K-9 is too difficult to get past and choose an easier target. On the other hand, the stalker may be convinced that the principal may enter or exit at the doors where the highly visible K-9s are posted. This could, in fact, be a diversion so that the principal can use another entrance.

CCTV CAMERA

2 WAY MIRROR

K-9

Three examples of security measures that work well together.

CHAPTER III

THE USE OF K-9S WITH ELECTRONIC SECURITY DEVICES

THE NEED FOR LAYERS OF PROTECTION

In the security field, it is not unusual to see the various options compared with each other as to effectiveness, liability, responsibility, deterrent level, ease of bypass and so on. Although each industry can cite statistics in its favor, every one of them will agree that the more options you choose to apply to your situation, the better prepared you will be. Therefore, a person who uses a K-9 and has barred windows and doors, a safe room, an electronic security system, a two-way security mirror, a closed-circuit TV, and a firearm is better off than the person who chooses only the firearm or the security system.

Since your first desire is to deter the criminal, you will accomplish this task more easily if the criminal sees several security measures in place. If the job is too risky, the perpetrator will likely head for an easier target.

Your best bet is to implement some measures that are obvious—such as security cameras, mirrors, iron bars and security K-9s—with others that are not so obvious, i.e., safe room, firearm, backup power source and cellular phone.

ELECTRONIC SECURITY DEVICES AND K-9s

Electronic security devices work particularly well in conjunction with K-9s, if the game plan is well thought out before implementation.

An audible alarm tone can be used in the training of the dog. When the alarm is sounded, the dog goes into action. This is nothing more than an electronic command, taught by a knowledgeable trainer. The dog is taught the appropriate response to the tone, a response that may be to apprehend, bark and hold or to knock down and hold. The alarm can be sounded by a panic button of the pen type (shown on page 45) or the scream of a siren or alarm bell when a motion detector or infrared sensor has signaled the presence of a perpetrator. The tone can even be high frequency and barely detectable to the human ear.

The use of the K-9 with electronics is accomplished when each has its own area of operation. For instance, K-9s may be used outside and electronics inside or vice versa. In some situations, K-9s may be used as the final protection with a firearm, such as in a bedroom, and the rest of the house or office may be protected by electronics. In some situations a combination of motion detectors or passive infrared detectors with K-9s may be used in close proximity to each other as long as each element has its own space. The two cannot be used directly together, as it is obvious that the electronics would be activated by the motion and body heat of the K-9s.

The following are just a few examples illustrating how K-9s and electronics can be used in conjunction with each other. In these instances, with the exception of the pen (a panic button, which is activated by a human), the electronics are used to detect, while the handler-dog team is used to apprehend and detain the perpetrator.

ELECTRONIC SECURITY DEVICES

In recent years, there have been incredible advances in the electronic security field. Those implementing security for businesses

When the business owner presses the panic button on the pen, an alarm tone is sounded and the dog comes running, ready for action.

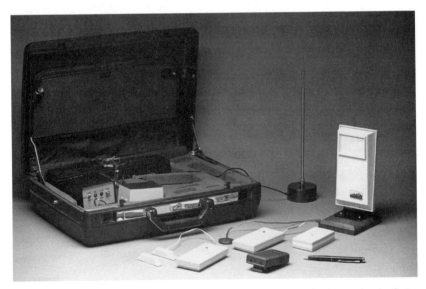

Intersector—RF—Indoor Protection System, courtesy of Executive Protection Institute, Berryville, Virginia.

have found that multiple layers of security provide the most effective coverage.

Another very effective combination of K-9 and electronics is realized when the perpetrator is thought to be an insider. In this case, whether the thief is an employee or janitor, the K-9's ability to detect or deter is diminished by the thief's access to the business and the thief's awareness of security measures.

Electronics can be used in a number of situations. In the following examples, one can see how the electronics are used to detect while the handler-dog teams are used to detain the suspects. These examples demonstrate how security measures can work in harmony with each other.

Pen with Panic Button

A husband and wife owned and operated a jewelry store located in a shopping center. After being robbed at gunpoint several times, they decided to implement several security measures. Their security consisted of closed-circuit TVs, a monitored security system, a protection-trained security K-9 and a special transmitter pen with a built-in panic button. The next time a suspicious-looking character entered the store, the wife made a simple gesture that appeared as though she had just depressed the button at the end of the pen. The pen, in actuality, transmitted a tone to her husband who was working in the back room with the K-9 nearby. He instantly responded with the dog. His arrival with the K-9 on the scene caused the suspicious-looking individual to exit the store promptly.

PORTABLE PROTECTION TECHNOLOGY

by Professor John I. Kostanoski, CST

Professor Kostanoski is an associate professor in the Department of Criminal Justice at the State University of New York, College of Technology, at Farmingdale. He is the coauthor of Security and

Loss Control *(Macmillan) and* Introduction to Security and Loss Control *(Prentice-Hall). He is a consultant to the National Institute of Justice, U.S. Department of Justice.*

The following devices are easy to operate, take less than five minutes to set up and even less time to remove, and they can be used in a variety of settings indoors and outdoors.

INDOOR SYSTEM: HOW IT WORKS

A wireless sensor detects the presence of a person and transmits a radio frequency signal to a receiver housed in an attaché case. This signal is retransmitted to a pager-receiver carried by a security person, or the signal is used to activate a siren. The signaling process takes seconds to complete. There are five types of sensors that are standard equipment on the portable indoor system: hand-held transmitter, executive pen transmitter, detector cell, magnetic actuated switch and passive infrared detector. This transmitter can be hidden in a soft pack of cigarettes. It produces a silent alert when its user is in a threat situation. It does so unobtrusively.

Applications

Hospital Nurse: A female nurse had been receiving threatening phone calls. She informed security that she was leaving for the day. As she approached her car, a stranger appeared and threatened her. She activated a hand-held transmitter in her coat pocket whose signal was received by a security officer on patrol. He responded in seconds.

Police: Narcotics officers were planning to make a buy from and subsequently arrest a drug dealer. The drug dealer specified the location for the transaction, which was to be a certain street corner. The buyer was provided with a hand-held transmitter cleverly disguised inside a soft pack of cigarettes. The buyer completed the transaction, pulled out his pack of cigarettes and in doing so alerted the stake-out team to make an arrest.

DETECTOR CELL

A momentary type switch can be placed under any object that weights at least two ounces. Removing or lifting the object activates the cell. Computer terminals, typewriters, books and even drawings, for example, can be protected with detector cells. Also known as a "theft button."

Application

University: A major university had suffered substantial losses of computer terminals. To put an end to these losses, detector cells were placed under those models known to have a high resale value. Shortly thereafter security received a signal that a terminal was being lifted. They responded and caught the thief. This is another instance where portable protection technology has enabled security to react instantly and witness a criminal act.

MAGNETIC ACTUATED SWITCH

This is a switch that consists of two separate units mounted in a fixed position (door jam, window frame, desk drawer frame) opposing the magnet, which is fastened to a moving door, window or desk drawer. When the door, window or desk drawer is opened, the magnet moves with it and away from the activated switch, thereby removing the force holding the switch closed, and so it opens. The change in the switch's position activates the transmitter.

Application

Business Office: Someone was entering an office and stealing items from desks. The door and desks were temporarily protected with magnetic activated switches. An employee entered the office after hours and triggered the magnetic activated switch on the door. Security was alerted and dispatched an officer to wait outside the office. The employee then opened a desk drawer, triggering another switch. Security walked in on the employee, who was caught in the act of stealing.

PASSIVE INFRARED DETECTOR

This battery-operated (9V transistor type) detector takes in what a human sends out, infrared energy or what we know as temperature. Because it *receives* and does *not emit* energy, the term "passive" is used. The detector operates in much the same way as our eyes, which see light, specifically, the visible light portion of the electro-magnetic spectrum. The detector "sees" the infrared portion of this same spectrum. The detector continuously monitors the infrared energy or temperature of everything within its field of view, and as long as the particular room's or zone's background temperature remains constant, nothing happens. If someone enters the detector's field of view, the difference in a human being's body temperature will cause the detector to activate a Radio Frequency (RF) transmission.

The detector is sometimes mounted on the ceiling, camouflaged as a smoke detector. It creates an invisible screen that surrounds a valuable object. A thief moving into this invisible screen to reach the object sets off the detector. Some models may also be used with a mirror. They can "see" infrared energy reflected in a mirror and thus can offer additional investigative-surveillance and personal protection applications.

APPLICATION

Corporate Espionage: An international corporation suspected that their computer tapes were being copied. A portable passive infrared detector detected entry into the computer room after normal business hours. It also detected re-entry into the computer room five hours later. Apparently cleaning personnel entered the computer room, took the tapes to be copied and then returned them.

OUTDOOR SYSTEM: HOW IT WORKS

A sensor (outdoor passive infrared motion detector) senses movement and transmits an RF signal to a receiver housed in an attaché case. This signal is retransmitted to pager-receivers carried by security personnel or the signal is used to activate a siren. The signaling process takes only seconds to complete. Standard equipment includes two outdoor passive motion detectors.

PASSIVE INFRARED MOTION DETECTOR

This battery-powered (three AA 1.5V) detector can operate during the day or night and can "see" the infrared energy emitted by a person or object in motion. It observes this energy through a line of sight, and it is weatherproof for outdoor use. It is designed to operate for two years before its batteries need to be replaced.

Application

Executive Protection: During a personal protection assignment, a principal—in this case a well-known political leader—parked his limousine and entered a restaurant to attend a luncheon meeting. Personal protection specialists placed outdoor passive infrared detectors around the car. If anyone attempted to plant or conceal a bomb on the car, the protection team would have been notified in seconds to counteract the attempt.

CONCLUSION

Criminal justice agencies and private security firms will redouble their emphasis on the recruitment, development and retention of quality personnel. As with other professions, technology is finding widespread use as a tool to aid security personnel in meeting increased demands for their services. As you can see in the previous examples, there are many instances where electronics can be used to detect the perpetrator. This is a valuable addition to the K-9 security team, especially in cases where it is suspected that the perpetrator is an insider.

CHAPTER IV

THE RIGHT K-9 TEMPERAMENT FOR YOUR NEEDS

Temperament is the most important consideration in selecting a potential security K-9. Temperament is also one of the least explored and understood aspects of the makeup of the dog. One definition of temperament is, "The manner of thinking, behaving and reacting; characteristic of a specific dog."

Temperament is so important because it is not a changeable factor. The dog is born with certain traits that we tend to refer to as "personality" (the totality of distinctive traits of an individual) or disposition. Trainers refer to the individual dog's traits as that dog's temperament. Any time that you choose a dog for a specific task, temperament is of the utmost importance. Just as you would not choose any old horse to race in the Kentucky Derby, you would be ill-advised to just randomly choose a dog for your protection. Your chances of being successful with a random choice are slim to none.

When you have a specific requirement for your protection dog, such as patrol work, area protection, VIP security or shop mascot, it becomes crucial that the dog's temperament fits the job description. This may mean that the dog needs to be antisocial in some cases or extremely mild mannered in others. In general, it is best to let a professional trainer help you choose your dog or puppy. This is a good idea because it takes a trained eye to spot subtle differences in temperament. Also, a dog professional, that is, one who spends the majority of his or her time with these dogs is more aware of potential pitfalls and will ask the necessary questions of a prospective buyer to help prevent problems down the line.

WHAT DOES "HARD" OR "SOFT" DOG MEAN?

"Hard" or "soft" are terms used by trainers to describe a dog's willingness to fight. When put in a defensive situation, the dog will respond by *fight* or *flight.*

A *hard* dog is one that will not back down. This dog is not easily intimidated by noise, novel objects or stick hits or kicks. A hard dog, in fact, will bite harder if the stick is used. Sticks are not meant to hurt the dog, but rather to simulate aggression and teach the dog how to deal with pressure. Sticks are padded or made of a lightweight reed material. A *soft* dog, on the other hand, is a dog who may put up a good defensive front. The dog may display extremely aggressive facial and body language such as showing teeth, lunging forward, barking and growling, but will likely back down when put under pressure. Some dogs will back down immediately when they see that the bluff of snarling and barking does not work. The soft dog may suddenly show signs of intimidation by laying back the ears or lowering the head and tucking the tail. Other soft types will bite, but will be backed down by a decoy who puts on too much pressure with the stick or fights more than the dog can handle. A soft dog will drop off of the bite when pressured. The dog may be soft because of a lack of drive, a low temperament or a lack of self-confidence learned as a result of prior improper handling by the owner or trainer.

If you are purchasing an adult *trained* dog, it is best to have your own licensed trainer evaluate the dog and decoy for the dog. This is

"Soft" eyes. This dog shows the typical characteristics of a social, nonthreatening canine. Head is held level, eyes are soft and receptive, ears are held in a casual, yet submissive, posture.

Before testing a dog who is known to be aggressive, have the owner attach two sturdy leashes and collars. A second trainer can hold one leash in order to protect the tester. If a trainer isn't available, you can use a tree or pole to secure the leash.

because a soft dog can be made to look better than it is if the decoy knows how to work without putting the dog into avoidance (that is, avoiding the circumstance by refusing to do the work). If you, as the buyer, can have your own decoy evaluate the dog, it will be a much more accurate evaluation.

THE TEMPERAMENT SCALE

The temperament scale is set up to more easily define the behavior patterns of the dog. Each individual dog is given a number from 1 to 10 based on the characteristics the dog displays. Every dog will fall between 1 and 10. If the dog seems to display some traits from both numbers, for instance 8 and 9, we would rate this dog an $8^1/_2$.

In this case, 10 is not the best, but rather the most dominant and assertive. The higher the dog is on the scale, the more likely a protection candidate this is with the exception of the 10, who is far too dominant to accept a subservient role to a human handler. To really understand how to rate a dog on the scale takes years of experience with various dogs. Only the experienced eye can quickly see the characteristics that will determine the rating.

TEMPERAMENT CHART

1–3: SEVERE PROBLEMS

1—Mental, Physical and/or Emotional Retardation

This dog, as a result of extreme trauma, early illness or genetic factors, is severely retarded. In many cases, there will be physical problems that may be noted at the same time. *This dog cannot learn.* There will be no retention of command, correction or praise. Many times these dogs have been saved at birth through human intervention, only to be kept alive with the aid of a lot of medical attention and constant owner care. Many of these dogs have to be carried from place to place, as they cannot find their way out of the house or to the food dish by themselves. The 1 on the scale is *untrainable.*

2 and 3—Therapy Cases
This dog can be helped to some degree with consistent therapy and training. The dog should have a complete examination and blood panel with a veterinarian to ensure that everything possible is done to help the dog medically.

2—Neurotic (Extreme Aggressive)
This is a genetic and possibly a medical problem. This dog has an extremely low stress threshold, probably responding with fight or flight reflexes to any stress, such as loud noises or strangers. This dog may shake to an extreme degree and a correction applied in training may send this dog into an uncontrolled panic attack. This dog is extremely dangerous to have around, especially with children, as it will react when startled or hurt by biting before thinking. You may see submissive body language coupled with aggressive behavior. *This is the classic fear-biter.*

3—Neurotic (Extremely Excitable)
This is likely a genetic problem; it could be the result of poor breeding. This dog will not sit still, and has trouble retaining commands. It will have little, if any, eye contact and will be in constant motion. Just as with hyperactive children, this dog may be able to be treated with medication, diet or other conditioning methods, which will create a better quality of life.

4–6: BALANCED, TRAINABLE DOGS

4—Balanced (Unmotivated)
This dog is aloof. This dog has the ability to retain commands, but is unmotivated and has little drive to do anything for the handler.

Such an animal may work for food reward, being primarily motivated for self-interest. This dog may be happy-go-lucky but lazy, and does not require a great deal of attention. This personality does not particularly care to play or chase a ball and would rather be alone. This dog's eye contact is minimal (approximately 25 percent).

5—Balanced (Average Motivation)

This is an average, sociable dog. Such a dog greets you with interest, and is not defensive. While not overly exuberant, this dog enjoys chasing a ball, but will tire of the game in time and get involved in something else or go lie down. This is a *very good* dog with children. Commands are accepted easily and without anxiety, with the dog displaying an even and balanced motivation to work. Eye contact will be around 30 to 40 percent.

6—Balanced (Good Motivation)

This dog is a great candidate for Obedience Trials or narcotics detection, search and rescue and similar activities if it possesses a good nose. It is *very social*. Greeting people with a high head, bright eyes and a sniffing nose, this type of dog displays a joyous attitude. The animal is highly motivated, and will chase a ball endlessly. This dog works well for all types of motivation, i.e., food, toy, praise. Eye contact is around 50 percent. This dog makes a good mascot and an adequate alarm dog, and its bark is generally an excited bark and not one based on defense.

7–9: BALANCED (PROTECTIVE/DEFENSIVE)

7—Balanced (Mildly Defensive)

This dog is pretty happy-go-lucky, but slightly leery of people, and shows some possessive behavior of toys, owners and home. Moderately Prey-driven, this dog's vocal aggression is high, which makes for a natural alarm and deterrent. However, this dog will be unsure when pressed to stand its ground. This dog is social, but watchful. Eye contact will be in the 60 to 70 percent range. This dog will go to Level 1 protection only. It is a good alarm dog, mascot or dual-purpose dog.

8—Balanced (Defensive)

This dog is a dominant type, but will adjust easily into a sub-servient role with the right handler. This dog displays good Prey Drive and can easily move from Level 1 to Level 2 and 3 protection where bite work is involved. It has a *very good balance of Prey and Defense Drives and, therefore, makes the best choice for shop protection, personal and family protection and VIP security.* This dog is naturally defensive with nonfamily members, yet not overly so. It is not looking for a confrontation and will not go into a defensive mode naturally, unless provoked or called into action. Eye contact will be around 70 to 80 percent; body language will be slightly stiffer than temperament 7, and will be poised for quick action.

9—Balanced (Extremely Defensive)

This dog is *very dominant* and pack-oriented. Although desiring to be the boss, it will submit to a handler who is dominant enough to impress the dog. This dog has an extremely high Defense Drive and will make an excellent patrol dog, area protection dog or police dog. This dog is too defensive to have in a shop or a social environment. Eye contact will be direct and 80 to 90 percent. This dog is unapproachable by strangers and does not trust easily. The handler has to have an assertive personality in order to command this dog's respect. This is done over time and bonding with the dog.

10—Untrainable: Alpha (Offensively Aggressive)

This is the alpha dog. *This dog will die before submitting to anyone.* The best you could hope for with this dog is a stand-off with a human handler who also has an alpha attitude. This dog will bite its own handler, is not social and, therefore, makes a good area pro-tection dog *only.* Handle with extreme care! *Not recommended.*

This dog is a walking lawsuit. If not destroyed, it must be kept under strict confinement and total control, utilizing leash, collar, muzzle and locked dog run. This dog should **never** be put in a social setting such as a shop or protection assignment in a home environment.

This dog will give 90 to 100 percent eye contact. It will give a direct, cold stare, rigid body and offensive appearance.

TEMPERAMENT TESTING

Temperament testing is the act of evaluating and reading the dog—the process whereby you take note of the dog's responses to its environment, stress and other tests that you set up. The dog's responses are noted and judged individually as well as together. This will leave you with an opinion of the dog. After testing many dogs, you will find that they will fall into groups based on similarities. This is why we use the number system. Before long, an experienced trainer can assign a number to a dog within five to ten minutes of meeting that dog.

PURPOSE OF EVALUATION

The reason that we need to know what kind of temperament the dog has is two-fold. The first reason is simply to know whether the dog will be good for the job. The second reason is so that we may train correctly. We need to know how dominant a handler is required and whether the dog is shy, bold or unmotivated. We also need to know what motivates the dog to work so that we can get the best effort from our hard work and training.

APPROACHING THE DOG

In order to do an evaluation you must be able to approach the dog and take the leash. You should already know if the dog is trained or untrained. You should know if there has ever been an unintended bite inflicted on a stranger, veterinarian or any other person.

It is a good idea not to rely on the say-so of a stranger. If you attempting to test a dog you don't know, use the double-leash method.

Double Leash

Give the owner two leashes and training collars to put on the dog. Secure one leash to a tree or pole before accepting the second leash from the owner. With this system, you can ensure that the dog will not be able to attack and is safely restrained. Two trainers can work together in much the same fashion.

Evaluation

The first part of the evaluation involves noticing the dog's response to approach. With the dog on the leash, begin with a simple Sit-Stay exercise. Watch the dog's response to you. Is the dog:

1. Oblivious to you? Unaware of your presence and unresponsive.
2. Extremely shy? Rolling eyes and showing fear-aggression.
3. Extremely excitable? Orienting on everything and nothing.
4. Ambivalent? Aware and voice responsive, but not interested.
5. Happy-go-lucky? Not overly excited, confident, wagging tail.
6. Happy worker? Active, exploring, responsive, sniffing.
7. Confident? Good eye contact, tail up, good-natured.
8. Confident, but reserved? Willing, but watchful.
9. CONFIDENT? Defensive, but willing to work.
10. Uncontrollably aggressive? Full eye contact, poised for attack upon provocation.

Eye contact is the clearest reading of the dog's temperament. The more eye contact you receive, the easier the dog is to train—with the exception of the dog that tries to stare you down. *Body language* is another good indication of the dog's temperament. When you approach, is the dog afraid? Relaxed? Curious? Aggressive? Are its hackles up? Is the dog rigid? Does it try to run? Are its ears and tail up or down?

All of these things must be seen. With the dog moving quickly, you must take note quickly as well. Take the dog far enough away

Pinch lightly between the toes to determine pain sensitivity. The dog should not panic. Pulling away, making a face or whining is acceptable. *Do not do this with an aggressive dog.*

from the owner that it will not be able to run to the owner for protection.

If all goes well on the approach, take some time to make the dog comfortable with you before you continue. Talk in a high-pitched voice; you could scratch the dog's chest as a friendly gesture. Do not touch the dog on the head or top of the shoulders if there is the slightest chance of an aggressive response. A dog may interpret touching the head and shoulders as a dominant gesture. When you are both comfortable with each other, you are ready to start your testing.

TESTING THE DOG

You will now need to test the dog for the various things that will be important to you in training. You need to know how responsive the dog is to praise and to correction and how quickly the dog will pick up on a command. You should now know if the dog is noise-, hand- or kick-shy (possible previous abuse), and how distractable the dog is likely to be.

In order to evaluate all of these things, start out with a simple sitting exercise. Do not use "Stay" in this exercise, as your goal is to see how long it will take the dog to figure out that staying is required. You ask the dog to "Sit" and give praise and correction when necessary to keep the dog in position. Once the dog is staying in position you will then begin to pace back and forth in front of the dog (approximately 3 feet) in a half circle. Typically the dog will alert and pay attention to you now, because in "dog language" this is a dominant act. Note if the dog responds to this by giving you submissive, neutral or dominant body posture. There are many other things that you will need to note about the dog while conducting this exercise. As an example:

DOG'S NAME: "THOR" AGE: 18 MONTHS BREED: GERMAN SHEPHERD DOG

1. HOW DOES THOR RESPOND TO VERBAL PRAISE?
Excites _____ Calms ____ Indifferent to praise ___ Not trusting ___

2. HOW DOES THOR RESPOND TO CORRECTION?
Responds instantly ___ Afraid of correction ___ Becomes defensive to correction ___

3. HOW DOES THOR RESPOND TO COMMANDS?
Willing to work ___ Responds from prior training ___ Oblivious to commands ___ Becomes afraid when given a command ___ Defensive when given command ___

4. HOW DOES THOR RESPOND TO TRAINING IN GENERAL?
Stubborn ___ Aggressive ___ Willing ___ Distracted ___ Happy-go-lucky ___

5. WHAT PERCENTAGE OF EYE CONTACT IS THOR GIVING YOU?
0–25% ___ 25–50% ___ 50–75% ___ 75–95% ___ 95–100% ___

6. WHAT IS THOR'S BODY LANGUAGE TELLING YOU?
Stares straight into eyes ___ Relaxed body ___ Submissive ___ Fearful/anxious ___ Aggressive ___

7. HOW LONG DOES IT TAKE TO TEACH THOR THE SIT/STAY?
(Attention span, learning rate) Sits quickly and stays ___ Takes a few times to get the idea ___ Stubborn/unwilling ___ Defensive ___ Short attention span ___

Before you complete the test, you will need to evaluate the dog's stress level. This is also known as testing the dog's nerves. The dog's reactions may be caused by genetic predisposition or they may be caused by the environment the dog has been subjected to. In some cases, it will be a combination of both.

Noise Shyness

Take a magazine or file folder and slap it against your leg. If the dog jumps back, throws its head or squints the eyes, ask the owner if the dog has been disciplined with a newspaper or magazine. You will have a hard time doing any kind of protection work with a fearful dog.

Hand and Foot Shyness

Take your hand and bring it down over the dog's head as if you were going to strike and stop just short of touching the dog. Does the dog flinch? Jump away? Squint? If the dog hits the ground, you will know the dog has probably been hit. If you have any doubts, ask the owner about the response. Bring your foot out in a kicking motion toward the dog; do *not* make contact. Does the dog shy? Jump away? Flinch? If the dog throws the rear to the side and jumps away, you will know this dog's probably been kicked. Ask the owner about this response.

Touch Sensitivity

Depending on the shyness of the dog on the first two tests, you will test the dog for touch sensitivity by one of two methods. If the dog appears to be overly sensitive, pinch the skin between the toes. Does the dog tolerate it? Pull Away? Scream? If you think that the dog is very tolerant, grab the extra skin over the shoulders or back and lift. Is the dog tolerant? Fearful? Does the dog become fear-aggressive?

Awareness Test

A good protection dog should be aware and curious of the sur-roundings. Use a squeaky toy, a clicker or your fingernails to make a clicking noise; hold the toy out of sight, behind your back. Make the noise. Does the dog look for the sound? You want to see the dog orient and try to locate it. If you move the sound, the dog should follow that sound wherever it goes.

After the dog is relaxed, have someone who hasn't been seen sneak behind a bush or vehicle making some noise from the hiding place. Does the dog alert on the noise? A good candidate for pro-tection at any level needs to be alert and aware.

Eye Contact

The more direct eye contact the dog gives you, the higher on the scale its temperament will be rated.

A direct stare into a dog's eyes is a challenge by a dominant individual. Your eye contact may be met by anything ranging from submission or indifference to all-out aggression. When you look into the dog's eyes, you will want to note the percentage of eye contact you receive, the other body language shown in addition to eye contact and whether or not the dog's eyes are soft and receptive or hard and defensive.

Eye contact is without a doubt your best way to read a dog. With practice you can predict behavior, read intentions, notice sharpness or softness and know whether you are going to be able to achieve your goals with this dog.

Warning: If the dog is an adult and known to be defensive, you should not do this without the dog being anchored to a person, pole or tree, for safety reasons. In case the dog tries to attack while being tested, the dog's range will then be limited.

TEMPERAMENT RATING

1–3 Little, if any, eye contact. Always looking away. Unaware of you or what you are doing. Will not meet your eyes. Will not hold your gaze. Very distracted. Always looking to escape.

4–6 25–50 percent eye contact. Will look at you and then look away. Relaxed, open, inquisitive about everything, not worried about you, not trying to escape, sniffing, curious.

7–9 60–90 percent eye contact. Will hold your gaze for long periods of time. May look away at times. May not look away at all. Not completely trusting. Attentive. May be rigid or relaxed. May appear defensive.

10 100 percent eye contact. Very cold eyes. Very rigid. **Intent to do bodily harm.**

PROTECTION SUITABILITY TEST

With the dog being held by the owner, three things are tested: *civil defense, prey drive and stress level.* Let's use Thor, an eighteen-month-old German Shepherd Dog, as an example:

CIVIL DEFENSE
Check the dog's willingness to be aggressive to the decoy or attacker.

1. Will Thor alert on a decoy at a distance?
2. Will Thor vocalize a threat to an obvious aggressor?
3. Will Thor maintain a threat at a close proximity?
4. Does Thor appear willing to bite when pressed?

PREY DRIVES
Check the dog's willingness to chase a prey object.

1. Will Thor chase a ball?
2. Will Thor chase a tug that is dragged on the ground?
3. Will Thor carry the prey object away?
4. Will Thor guard the prey?

NOISE AND TOUCH SHYNESS
Does Thor show extreme fear of loud noises or self-protection when being touched roughly? When the dog is subjected to the following situations, what reactions do you observe?

1. Shoot a starting pistol *at a distance*. Does the dog shy from the noise?
2. Bang a dish or other metal object nearby. Does Thor shy or jump away from the noise?
3. Pull the loose skin on the dog's back or flanks. Do you see a fear reaction?

Defense Drive is displayed when the dog focuses on the decoy who is not wearing any equipment. The facial display is a visible warning of the dog's intent.

Prey Drive is displayed by the dog's willingness to chase and bite a moving object, such as this puppy tug.

4. Wave your hand on stick over Thor's head. Does he jump back or flinch?

A dog must have good balance in all of these areas to make a good protection dog. The dog must show a good degree of natural Defense and Prey Drive in order to learn the proper response under command.

The should not show shyness or viciousness. You should find out if this dog has had previous experiences that put you at risk in training, such as biting a family member, veterinarian or other person for no apparent reason. If the dog has been *abused* by someone in early life, this dog will *not* be a good candidate because prior imprinting will ruin this dog's potential. The best dogs will be ones that you can start on a training program when they are young.

TEMPERAMENT = JOB DESCRIPTION

IF THEY RANK,	THEN THE BEST ASSIGNMENT IS:
6	**Alarm dog only.** Not defensive enough to be a protection dog.
7–7$\frac{1}{2}$	**Dual purpose dog:** ranch dog, store mascot, etc.

The dog that is going to be loose in an area where people come and go freely (who may stop and talk to or pet the dog) must have a fairly low temperament score as protection dogs go. This dog's primary function is to be a visual deterrent, and secondarily, to be an alarm system. As an example, ranch dogs are typically used to bark an alarm as people drive onto the property. They are often used around the horse barns and trailers to warn of intruders.

Mascots are used in a variety of businesses and are usually found walking freely around the premises. If they are large, they are used as a visual deterrent; if they are small, they can act as a little alarm to sound a warning of someone approaching, especially after hours.

8–8½   **Black tie K-9:** executive/VIP security, hotel and hospital security, jewelry store, gift shop, etc.

The dog involved in security work using handler-dog teams in social situations needs to be extremely well-behaved. This is also true of the dog who spends the day in a jewelry store, convenience store, gift shop, etc. This dog is going to be expected to accept the comings and goings of large numbers of strangers and, at the same time, to be alert to danger.

9–9½   **The terminator:** security patrol, police patrol, etc.

The patrol dog has to have a highly defensive attitude, as this dog deals with the bad guys in the urban jungle. This dog has to be a *hard* dog who can dish it out and take it. This dog's main function is to protect the handler and to assist in apprehension of suspects.

9½–10   **Property protection:** area or vehicle protection, protection of assets.

The area protection dog needs to be independent and antisocial. This dog's sole responsibility is to keep people out of the area that the dog is protecting. Because area dogs work without the assistance of humans, it is essential that they have attitudes just as aggressive *with or without* a handler present.

CONCLUSION

It is imperative that you are cognizant of the importance of the dog's temperament when you choose a K-9 for your business. If you were to make the wrong choice, you would be running the risk of having a dog who was either too aggressive or not aggressive enough for the job. Either of these mistakes could be very dangerous to the handler or the patrons of the business

FACTORING IN PREY DRIVE AND CIVIL DEFENSE DRIVE

When you are trying to get an accurate reading on temperament of a particular dog, it is important to remember that you are not judging the dog's temperament according to Prey or Defense Drive. *When we are judging temperament, we are rating the dog on assertiveness.* This means the dog's ability to stand up for itself or assert its own will over that of another. We may say we are *judging the dominance* of the dog, which will reflect *its ability to control* a situation or a person or animal.

In contrast, the Prey Drive is the drive for the dog to chase and catch. This is evidenced in dogs who will endlessly play ball or a game of tug-of-war. When protection training the security dog, we use this drive in teaching the dog to bite. Do not make the mistake of deciding that the dog with high Prey Drive must be more dominant than a dog with low Prey Drive. Consider all of the hounds and retrievers who love to chase and tug. *Dominance and Prey Drive are not connected.*

To the contrary, the defense drive can easily be linked to temperament. The Defense Drive is the drive used when a dog protects territory, people or possessions. It is very easy to figure that the dog who shows the most teeth or growls the most is the most dominant. Not so. Many times, the dog who makes the biggest display of facial and vocal aggression will be the last dog to actually bite you. By contrast, dogs who will not display aggression may simply stare at you before biting.

The best protection dogs have a combination of high temperament (stable), balanced Prey and Defense Drives (50/50, 60/40 or 40/60) and good nerves (genetic).

THE HANDLER'S TEMPERAMENT

It is also important to note that a handler should have some idea about his or her own temperament. The ability to be assertive and controlling is a very large factor in the success of your training with a protection dog. A protection dog must have an assertive nature; but you must be more assertive by nature than your dog if you expect to control the dog.

Dogs are much better at assessing temperament than we are, and much quicker at reading us. Therefore, you *must* be cognizant of your abilities. For example, if you would consider your own temperament to be a 7, don't buy a dog who is a 9.

CHAPTER V

SELECTING A BREED AND CHOOSING YOUR PUPPY

WHY IS THE BREED IMPORTANT?

When you are looking for a dog specifically for security, you will need to select a dog that has the following traits:

1. **The dog must desire to stay near the owner.** The dog cannot protect you if straying or running away. If overly excited by the scent of another animal or possessing a tendency to run off, the dog won't be any good to you.
2. **The dog must be social, but defensive enough to be aware of the actions of strangers toward the owner.** A dog that trusts everyone is not a good choice. The dog should be defensive enough to be taught to sound the alarm or threaten as a minimum security measure.
3. **The dog must be controllable.** In both Obedience and protection scenarios, the dog must be voice responsive.

Some breeds will "tune out" when they are preoccupied with another animal.

4. **The security dog must be large and sturdy enough to deter a would-be perpetrator.** With the exception of the alarm dog, the security dog should weigh over fifty pounds and, in the case of the man-stopping patrol dog, the closer to one hundred pounds, the better.

Because of these traits, your field of prospective breeds will be narrowed quite a bit. This is because, over time, people have bred dogs for various tasks and some of the breeds historically do not make suitable candidates for a particular job. They are wonderful at what they were bred to do, but the very traits that they need for *their work* may conflict with the traits needed for a security dog.

A good example is the Siberian Husky. Many people expect the Siberian to act like a German Shepherd Dog. People falsely believe that since both breeds have that "wolfy" look they should be similar in other traits. This is far from the case. Siberian Huskies were bred for sled pulling and, therefore, are great endurance runners. A personal protection dog or security K-9 must stay by the owner's side. The Siberian Husky is notorious for running away.

Bird dogs such as the Labrador and Golden Retrievers are far too social and trusting by nature. They were bred with soft mouths so that they would be less likely to bite down hard on birds. These are opposite traits than are desired in a security K-9. It is therefore rare to find a retriever who can perform as a security K-9. There are some exceptions in all breeds, but in general, you will find most of your likely candidates in the Working Group and Herding Group as well as a few in the Terrier Group. These groups are classified as such with the American Kennel Club.

This is not to say that all of the Working dogs are good prospects for protection. As previously stated, the Nordic breeds are not. Nor are some of the Herding breeds or terriers. Our best recommendation is to check carefully into any breed that you are considering for your specific security needs.

THE ROLE OF GENETICS IN SELECTING A DOG

The temperament of the dog is primarily created through genetic makeup. When two dogs are bred, they *each* give the puppies genes that produce various traits and temperaments. Although puppies in the same litter will share quite a few common characteristics, no two animals will truly be identical. As we know, in humans even twins who appear identical still have variations in personality.

We do know that, in general, we will have a better chance of acquiring a puppy with the proper temperament for security work if the dog is from a background of dogs who were worked in security, police, protection or one of the European sports that involves protection work. *The buyer should understand that temperament testing the litter is still recommended,* as even an outstanding breeding of two Working dogs, can double on a recessive gene or two that creates a soft temperament or even an overly aggressive or unstable temperament.

Likewise, we may get a dog with an unusually high assertive temperament for its breed through recessive genes (inherited characteristics that are not obvious in a given dog, but that may be passed on to offspring). From time to time you may find an unlikely breed, such as a Labrador Retriever, Standard Poodle or Dalmatian that has the proper drives to do the work. Even so, you will find 95 percent of the working quality dogs will come out of good working backgrounds.

There are many *physical conditions* that can limit the dog's working ability. The buyer should research the breed he or she is interested in purchasing and pay attention to all of the known physical problems with regard to this breed. Talk not just with one, but with many breeders and veterinarians who are very familiar with the breed. Some examples of special conformation or medical problems that can hinder working ability are:

1. Hip Dysplasia—a genetic defect where the ball and socket of the hip joint do not fit together properly. Can result in moderate to severe lameness and increased arthritis.

2. Several breeds can be predisposed to elbow dysplasia as well as luxating patellas (slipping stifles).
3. Von Willebrand's disease—a free-bleeding disorder that is inherited.
4. Spinal problems related to defects in the cartilage appear in several of the Working breeds.
5. Extra-short muzzles can make breathing difficult, especially during bite work. When a dog bites, it must breathe through the nose.
6. Overly large jowls can also pose a problem during bite work, as dogs may constantly bite their own lips.
7. Dogs with excessively large bones can be lacking in agility and mobility.
8. Inverted eyelids can scratch the dog's eyes and create constant tearing, irritation and even blindness.

ADOPTING A PUPPY OR DOG

Another option that you have with regard to selection is adoption. There are many wonderful dogs who have been abandoned by their former owners. You can find them in every county animal shelter. Another excellent place to look for a specific breed is the rescue service for that chosen breed. If, for instance, you are looking for a German Shepherd Dog you can call your local German Shepherd Dog club and ask if they have a rescue service.

What a breed rescue service does is alert local animal shelters that it will adopt an animal of that breed. The rescue service will then attempt to place the dog in a good home. Dogs that come through breed rescue get a lot of individualized attention.

The service will typically allow the dog to be tested by a professional. You will have to fully explain what you intend to do with the dog, as the service will not want the dog to go to a fence-dog situation unless they feel that the dog is so antisocial that this is the only use for the dog. You may come across a dog who has been abused or has severe behavioral problems that have to be overcome. Most rescue services would put down such an antisocial animal, as they would not want to put such a dog in a stranger's hands. If you explain that the dog will be a mascot in a store, or that you plan to take the dog to work and back home again for personal protection, there may be a dog for you, as most breed clubs simply want to make sure that the dog will be well cared for and not exploited.

Some professional trainers may have a relationship with the operator of the local Humane Society or animal shelter where they can be kept informed of any exceptional dogs who are abandoned. This type of relationship will help everyone concerned. It gives the animal a much better chance of being adopted, the prospective owner and trainer a good dog to work with, and it helps the Humane Society or shelter place more animals.

The dog used for protection does not have to be a purebred to be effective. It does, however, have to possess the right temperament for the work. You are much more likely to find a Shepherd and Doberman mix that can do the work than you are an Afghan and Irish Setter mix.

The difference between adopting a dog versus a puppy is that with a dog you can relatively see what you're getting. You can have a veterinarian and a trainer examine the dog and know what to expect as far as temperament and physical health. With regard to a puppy, things are not this simple. You will not be able to predict how the pup will turn out physically or psychologically beyond what can be determined presently. If you don't have access to a pedigree or background information, you cannot make an educated decision. Adopting a young puppy without this information is a gamble.

BREEDS

Choosing a breed is somewhat like choosing a car. The first thing that usually attracts people is appearance. Everyone has a different idea as to what is attractive. Some people like the lean, sleek lines of the Doberman Pinscher. Still others like the massive size of the Rottweiler, Dogue de Bordeaux, Mastiff or Bullmastiff. There are certain people who enjoy the care it takes to keep a Bouvier des Flandres in good coat condition. The following breeds are just some of the potential candidates for the role of business security K-9. The breeds included are some of the best choices when the job calls for a dog that can apprehend a perpetrator. Of course, after a judgment is made regarding the appearance of the dog, you will need to "check under the hood" so to speak. What ability does the dog have to function as you desire? How much maintenance will be required? After these questions are asked and answered you will know if your choice is realistic. The following breeds are listed in random order.

ROTTWEILER

Today the Rottweiler is known as a German breed, as it is named after the town of Rottweil in Germany. This breed is, however, two thousand years old and was found previously in Italy where the Roman legions used them to heard livestock over the Alps and guard the weapons depots by night. Later, the Germans in Rottweil saved the breed from extinction by establishing a sound breeding program that emphasized the dog's physical soundness and working abilities, which include herding ability, protection skills and cart pulling.

Typical Rottweilers are neither shy nor overly aggressive. They bond closely to their family members and are known to follow the owner from room to room in the house, as they desire to lie at the feet of their loved ones. Rottweilers are very popular as personal protection dogs, as they are not excessive barkers or overly active. By the same token, they are not recommended for patrol purposes or job descriptions that require endurance, especially in the heat. They are most natural in the role of bodyguard. This breed should be Obedience trained at a young age, as they grow rapidly and may become willful without proper training and discipline.

Common health problems: Hip dysplasia, thyroid, Von Willebrand's disease and cataracts. Average life span is ten years.

Rottweiler, Ch. Tula's Barcez Golden Nugget owned by Doug and Bonnie Price. *Photo by Macias, courtesy of Windeville Rottweilers*

German Shepherd Dogs, Erle Vom Telgerpen Land, Sch III, Earl Vom Haus Hansing, Sch III, Ute Von den Jungen Hansen, Sch III and Bruno of Dair, Sch III, CD, owned by David Macias.
Photo by Macias, courtesy of Rosenholz German Shepherd Dogs

National (Parent) Breed Club: American Rottweiler Club, Secretary: Doreen LePage, 960 South Main Street, Pascoag, RI 02859.

GERMAN SHEPHERD DOG

A mountain dog with powerful hindquarters, as well as firm and correct forequarter angulation to match, combined with a plains dog having tremendous endurance and long, reaching gate, the German Shepherd Dog came to be as we know it today. The German Shepherd Dog, which originated in Germany, is over one hundred years old. Today the German Shepherd is found worldwide. With intelligence, mental stability, endurance, structural efficiencies, ability to scent, willingness to work, courage and trainability, the German Shepherd has become one of the most versatile breeds in the world.

Found in homes as companion dogs, leading the blind, doing search and rescue, working as police dogs, sniffing out drugs, herding sheep or just plain being the loyal companion of a child, the German Shepherd Dog is truly a dog like no other.

Possible Health Problems: Hip dysplasia, Cervical Vertebral Instability (CVI)—or "wobblers" generally occurs in older males, caused by pinched nerves in the rear of the dog. This is genetic and dog is unsuited for breeding (Ref: Dr. Beckie Williams, DVM & GSD breeder), colitis and other intestinal ailments and stomach sensitivities. To ensure a lack of any breed's inherited predisposition for these ailments, careful selection of the breeder is advised.

National (Parent) Breed Club: German Shepherd Dog Club of America, Inc., Secretary: Blanche Beisswenger, 17 West Ivy Lane, Englewood, NJ 07631.

BELGIAN MALINOIS

This breed is becoming very popular in the United States in the field of law enforcement. This is because the Malinois is constantly ready for action, with a seemingly endless supply of energy. The Belgian Malinois is also relatively free of physical problems (with the exception of occasional problems with epilepsy). This breed can be of use to a police department for more years than any other breed, as the Malinois breed is relatively free of hip dysplasia and CVI. Cervical Vertebral Instability—or "wobblers" generally occurs in older males and is caused by pinched nerves in the rear end of the dog. This is genetic and the dog is unsuited for breeding.

The Belgian Malinois should reflect the qualities of intelligence, courage, alertness and devotion to master. To their inherent aptitude as guardian of flocks should be added protectiveness of the person and property of their masters. Malinois should be watchful, attentive and always observant and vigilant with strangers, but not apprehensive. They should not show fear or shyness, nor show viciousness by unwarranted or unprovoked attacks. With those they know well, they are most affectionate, friendly, zealous of their attention and very possessive.

Because of their herding instinct, Malinois are very keen to movement, therefore to body language. Any move you make, they will pick up on. This is very important for puppies, since they regard the owner as the pack leader. Some puppies go through a growth period during which they may show either fear, shyness or aggressiveness. The owner who pets the pup excessively, hoping to convey reassurance, is actually transmitting fears from owner to pup, who is then being rewarded for shyness or aggressiveness. Ignoring the undesirable behavior and rewarding the good behavior will give the pup confidence. Malinois are handler oriented, but some are handler sensitive, which is what makes them so easy to train, as they are so willing to please. But, beware—the heavy-handed owner will very easily ruin such a dog, while the one who trains with motivation can have a "wonder" dog.

National (Parent) Breed Club: American Belgian Malinois Club, Secretary: Barbara Peach, 1717 Deer Creek Road, Central Valley, CA 96019.

Belgian Malinois, Ch. Etoile de la Counterpointe, HIC, owned by Daniele Daugherty.

Photo by D. Daugherty, courtesy of Crocs-Blancs Belgian Malinois

Belgian Sheepdog, Ch. Inchallah Kia Bear Sirdar, owned by Phyllis Davis and William Doyle.

Belgian Tervuren, Ch. Daradan's Expectation D'Mar, owned by Dara Wilcox.

Photo by J. Ludwig, courtesy of Daradan Belgian Tervuren

BELGIAN SHEEPDOG

In 1891 a veterinarian, Professor Adolphe Reul, gathered together shepherds and dog fanciers from around Brussels and Belgium to attempt to define and promote the native herding dog of Belgium. He found a medium-sized, prick-eared dog of similar type, though in many different colors. There were three coat types—short, long and harsh—which remain to this day. Although Professor Reul recommended breeding by coat type, coat color became the preferred choice, leading to four varieties of Belgian Shepherds. They are the Groenendael, the long-haired black dog known as Belgian Sheepdog in the United States; the Belgian Tervuren, a long-haired fawn or mahogany dog with a black overlay; the Belgian Malinois, a short-haired fawn dog; and the Laekenois, a harsh, curly coated fawn dog.

In 1959, the American Kennel Club separated the three varieties—Groenendael, Tervuren and Malinois—into separate breeds, naming the Groenendael the Belgian Sheepdog. The Laekenois is not yet recognized by the AKC, though several have been imported in recent years.

The ideal home for a Belgian Sheepdog is one in which the people devote a lot of attention and love to their dogs. Also, due to the Belgian's high intelligence and creativity, it is recommended that basic obedience training begin with a young puppy and early socialization is very important. A Belgian needs to be active both mentally and physically. They are definitely *not* couch potato dogs.

For some people, the Belgian's high energy level, demand for constant love and attention and sensitive nature are undesirable. Also, the Belgian's double coat does require regular grooming, which some owners do not have the time for or want to do.

The description of the personality of the Belgian Sheepdog breed is of the utmost importance in appreciating the breed. They should be stable, intelligent, and willing to meet new situations. The rapidity with which the Belgian learns and responds to the owner's every wish makes this breed a joy to train for whatever purpose, whether as an Obedience dog, show dog, herder, house pet, companion for children or the handicapped, or a guardian of the home.

Potential health problems: Hip dysplasia, seizures, thyroid deficiencies, skin allergies, flee allergies, auto-immune deficiencies and some eye problems. All reputable breeders should be testing for the following problems: the sire and dam of a litter should be OFA'd (cleared of hip dysplasia), have their eyes checked clear, thyroids checked, and that they not seizure or have littermates that seizure.

National (Parent) Breed Club: Belgian Sheepdog Club of America, Secretary: Phyllis Davis, 2530 Harbison Road, Cedarville, OH 45314.

BELGIAN TERVUREN

The Belgian Tervuren is a very intelligent breed, easily trained in various areas of expertise. Herding, Tracking, search and rescue, Obedience, protection and European sports are all areas in which they excel. Tervuren are typically willing to please and are very oriented toward being at the owner's side.

This breed possesses great endurance and agility and adapts well to all climates, from freezing weather to temperatures of 100-plus degrees. The Tervuren is lightweight enough to be an exceptional jumper and yet heavy enough to be forceful. It is extremely important to choose your breeder carefully, as some Tervuren can be skittish and shy. This trait should be avoided and puppies should be well socialized in order to prevent shyness toward strangers. This breed has a very high activity level, which also makes them excellent candidates for Obedience Trial work.

The Tervuren's coat is somewhat wash-and-wear, with regular brushing between baths. The major health concerns are hip dysplasia and epilepsy, although health problems are few in this breed and life spans average twelve to fifteen years.

National (Parent) Breed Club: American Belgian Tervuren Club, Inc., Secretary: Nancy Carman, 4970 Chinook Trail, Casper, WY 82604.

Doberman Pinscher

The Doberman Pinscher is a German breed developed by Louis Dobermann in the late 1800s. Although only one hundred years old, the Doberman breed has gained popularity quickly as a superb athlete, willing Obedience dog and courageous protector.

With the soaring popularity of the breed also came overbreeding that created many health problems and temperament deficiencies. Problems range from thyroid, Von Willebrand's disease, Cervical Vertebral Instability or "wobblers," which generally occurs in older males and is caused by pinched nerves in the rear end of the dog. This is genetic and the dog is unsuited for breeding; heart problems and low stress level that can result in fear biting.

The top breeders in the United States who compete in European Dog Sports that require strong nerves, a balanced temperament and a strong and physically sound Doberman typically import their breeding stock from Europe. They report that they import their stock because of the sound breeding policies in Europe, which produce the Dobermans that can compete at the top levels of the sport, i.e., Schutzhund, IPO and French Ring Sport.

On the whole, typical Dobermans are very family oriented. They are quick, energetic and willing to please. Most behavioral problems reported stem from the dog being isolated from the family. Negative attention is better than no attention at all. If ignored by their owners, Dobermans may bark, whine, chew or dig, or jump on doors or windows to get attention. It is *not true* that Dobermans turn on their masters. This is a media myth and has more to do with ill breeding than the breed itself.

National (Parent) Breed Club: Doberman Pinscher Club of America, Secretary: Judy Reams, 10316 N.W. 136th Place, Kirkland, WA 98034.

Doberman Pinscher, Aldercrest Danzig, Sch III, owned by Linda Calamia.
Photo by D. Sweeney, courtesy of Aldercrest Doberman Pinschers

Giant Schnauzer, Ch. Skansen's Quidame, owned by Sylvia Hammarstrom.
Photo by D. Wong, courtesy of Skansen Giant Schnauzers

GIANT SCHNAUZER

The Giant Schnauzer belongs to the Working Group and is bred for working and protection abilities. This breed makes an excellent family watchdog, taking the work quite seriously. Giant Schnauzers become very protective about their car, house and owner. Because of its size, it is recommended that the Giant gets basic Obedience training as a youngster in order to be well controlled as an adult. Protection work is instinctive with this breed, and with proper training and guidance, it can be quite formidable.

The Giant Schnauzer has a hard, wiry coat which is good for weather protection. They can live outdoors but, like most watchdogs, prefer to be inside with the family where they can do the most good, should it become necessary. There are two types of coats seen in the United States. The first is a hard, wiry coat the Germans originally intended the breed to have. This is a very easy coat to care for as the leg furnishings are sparse, and minimum grooming is needed. The other is a softer coat, with lots of hair on the legs and a profuse beard. This kind of coat obviously requires much more care; the hair on the legs tangles easily. This coat is, however, quite attractive and makes one think of a furry bear, which makes some people very fond of this, even though it is not correct strictly according to the Standard. If the dog is going to spend a lot to time outside where foxtails or mud exists, choosing the harder coat is important.

Regardless of the type of coat, this breed does not shed much, which is very convenient for an indoor pet. Also, because of its minimal shedding coat, children and adults allergic to dogs can very often tolerate the Schnauzer just like the Poodle.

The Giant Schnauzer is a very hardy animal with low instances of degenerative diseases and a long life if properly cared for. Like all large breeds, hip dysplasia is always possible.

Giant Schnauzers love any kind of unrestrained work like retrieving, jumping, attack work, barking on command and

Tracking (they have superb noses). They are not the best precision workers, as they get impatient with too much repetition, but with a good trainer, they make excellent competition Obedience dogs if properly motivated.

Like most dogs, the Giant Schnauzer is excellent with children if raised with them. This is very important, and it is not recommended for a family with young children to bring in an older dog not previously raised with children. However, if dogs are raised with children, they make terrific playmates. They will play all day, can be trained to pull the kids in carts and love to go swimming with them. Giant Schnauzers require a lot of exercise and attention as pups and young adults. However, once they have grown up, they are happy to just sleep next to you all day. Like any big dog, they should have at least thirty minutes to one hour of good exercise daily. If exercised properly, they are as good an apartment dog as any smaller breed.

National (Parent) Breed Club: Giant Schnauzer Club of America, Secretary: Dorothy Wright, 4220 S. Wallace, Chicago, IL 60609.

BOXER

The Boxer is the result of a Mastiff-type dog bred to a Bulldog. This has produced the characteristic short muzzle that resembles the Bulldog. This short muzzle has some drawbacks in protection work as the Boxer finds it difficult to pull enough air through its nose while biting to be able to sustain a long apprehension if a suspect resists. However, what the breed lacks in biting endurance it makes up for in courage and determination. A Boxer with characteristic temperament will not give up easily as the fighting drive will sustain this dog. This breed was originally bred for bull baiting and fighting and therefore has an abundance of prey drive and fighting instinct. Because of this strong will, the breed should be Obedience trained when young, with an emphasis on *positive* methods, keeping the training fun and enjoyable for this breed that is easily bored.

Boxer, Ch. Lynel's Heleva Good Lookin' Guy, owned by Margi Roberson.

Photo by Olan Mills, courtesy of Heleva Boxers

Bullmastiff, Ch. Roderic's Ropin' the Wind, owned by Carol R. Haddon.

Photo by J. Ludwig, courtesy of Roderic Bullmastiffs

Dogue de Bordeaux, "Bilbo" of Norris Place, owned by Steve and Wendy Norris.

Photo by W. Norris Williams, courtesy of Norris Place Dogue de Bordeaux

The correct appearance is a dog of medium size with strong limbs, a square build and a short, tight coat. This dog is also excellent traveling in the car with the owner, as it is not oversized. This breed can become cold easily because of the short, tight coat and therefore prefers to be indoors in cold weather.

This breed is very tolerant with children and loves to play the clown as center of attention. The Boxer desires to be a companion, wherever the owner may go. A lack of attention can easily cause this breed to become destructive or fence jump in order to get the attention sought.

Possible health problems: Heart, thyroid, hip dysplasia, cancer and colitis. Average life span is ten years.

National (Parent) Breed Club: American Boxer Club, Inc., Secretary: Barbara E. Wagner, 6310 Edward Drive, Clinton, MD 20735-4135.

BULLMASTIFF

The Bullmastiff was bred to knock down poachers and hold them until the master arrived to administer the appropriate punishment. To this day, Bullmastiffs learn quickly where humans bend (at the knees) and regularly practice their art of knockdown.

This is a very gentle breed, kind and forgiving. They are loving family dogs and will adjust to an active or sedate environment. They do not take heat well and must be kept cool with plenty of fresh water on hand in the summer months. Bullmastiffs, like other large breeds, should be trained young and be well socialized with children and other animals that are expected to cohabitate with them. They have very few behavioral problems around the house and barking is not a problem, as they are noted for a silent attack.

Potential health problems: Skin problems, cysts between the toes, and ear fungus. Be selective with this breed regarding the health of the parents and grandparents.

National (Parent) Breed Club: American Bullmastiff Association, Inc., Secretary: Mary Anne Duchin, Box 137D Burger Road, Melbourne, KY 41059.

DOGUE DE BORDEAUX

The Dogue de Bordeaux is a French breed of Mastiff. This breed is known as "the National Guard Dog of France." Hitler ordered all Bordeaux shot on sight in World War II as they were known to be extraordinarily protective of their families. Because of this, after World War II there were only three pairs of Bordeaux reported to be alive.

This breed's most natural protection skill is the takedown. In an altercation their natural style is to run close to the ground and spring at the adversary, hitting in the midsection with the head or chest. They then stand over the perpetrator, daring the person to move.

Even as puppies, the owners notice that the youngsters learn quickly that humans bend at the knees. They will use their body weight or paws to playfully bring down the owner to the ground at eye level with them. This is a breed that loves children and gets along well with other animals. They are know to be stubborn and slow to react to Obedience commands, although they react with lightning speed if they want to in their everyday lives.

Although sometimes difficult to breed, their overall health is generally good after eight weeks of age. Hip dysplasia is a problem with this breed as with all Mastiff-type dogs. This breed is slow to mature and not considered an adult in France until age three.

National (Parent) Breed Club: United States Bordeaux Club, Secretary: Bonnie Gordon, 29 Hemlock Hill Road, Jackson, NJ 08527.

BOUVIER DES FLANDRES

The Bouvier des Flandres was originally bred to work as an all-purpose farm dog. This breed was used to herd cattle, control vermin and guard the premises. The Bouvier was built for agility rather than speed.

The Bouvier is mild in temperament compared with other breeds such as the Rottweiler or Malinois. They are calmer and less "sharp" by nature and therefore make good house dogs. When looking for a good working line for security purposes, look for lines

Bouvier des Flandres, "Rouska", owned by Dave Barron.

Photo by D. Barron, courtesy of San Bernadino County Sheriff's Department

Akita, Ch. Asahi Yama No Hanashi, owned by Frank, Sylvia and Eric Thomas.

Photo by Vavra, courtesy of Chiheisen Akitas

American Staffordshire Terrier, Ch. Anthem's Walter J. Boldwin, owned by Guadalupe Bravo and Katrina Cliff.

Photo by J. Ludwig, courtesy of Anthem American Staffordshire Terriers

directly out of Germany or Holland, as many Bouviers are too mild-mannered and sedate for the work. Look for Schutzhund or KNPV titles in the dog's pedigree, as a good working-quality Bouvier is hard to find.

Grooming is a consideration when purchasing this breed. Frequent brushing is suggested, along with a monthly trip to the groomer.

Medically, the Bouvier is typically a very healthy breed, lacking the long list of potential health problems of many other breeds. The Bouvier's ears may be cropped at six to eight weeks of age, and this does require some follow-up care.

National (Parent) Breed Club: American Bouvier des Flandres Club, Inc., Secretary: Dianne Ring, Rte. 1 Box 201, Delaplane, VA 22026.

AKITA

The Akita was originally bred as a versatile hunting dog in Northern Japan. The breed was noted for its combination of good nature and courage. Akitas have a reputation for being aloof because they do not crave attention like some other breeds. Akita breeders would rather refer to them as "independent" because the breed will typically greet their owners with tails wagging and quickly go about their business of exploring or go and lie down under a shade tree. The Akita has also been described as stubborn, but again, breeders feel this is simply a sign of the same "independent" nature. The Akita may well understand what is being asked from the owner but may decide on a case-by-case basis.

Akitas have been used in police work, but are more commonly used for home or personal protection. This breed is instinctively protective and therefore it is essential that they be heavily socialized with large numbers of people as puppies. It is also recommended that they are trained young (prior to one year of age) so that Obedience is established before dominance sets in at one to two years of age. This breed, although independent, is sensitive to owner/handler correction and does not typically require severe correction. Akitas are much more willing to please when working with a kind, consistent handler.

Potential health problems: Hip dysplasia, bloat, PRA (Progressive Retinal Atrophy), thyroid, entropion.

National (Parent) Breed Club: Akita Club of America, Secretary: Barbara Hampton, 7729 Rio Vista Street, Las Vegas, NV 89131.

AMERICAN STAFFORDSHIRE TERRIER

The American Staffordshire Terrier was originally bred to be a fighting dog. This breed is rock-hard in appearance, with well-defined muscles. The Am Staff (as the breed is called) is fearless and alert by nature, taking readily to Obedience and making an excellent person protector and companion.

The greatest problem with this breed other than bad owners and negative media attention, is bad temperament usually caused by improper and irresponsible breeding. This is a strongly prey-driven dog and breeding should be carried out carefully to eliminate an unbalanced temperament. Because of the strong Prey Drive and strong physical abilities of this breed, it is not recommended that an adult American Staffordshire Terrier be brought into a home with preschool-age children. It is preferable to start with a young puppy that can be raised with children.

Potential health problems: Hip dysplasia, skin problems, allergies, ear infections and epilepsy. These problems are not extremely common to the breed but they are usually hereditary. Great care should be taken in researching your potential puppy's parents and genetic background before selection is complete.

National (Parent) Breed Club: Staffordshire Terrier Club of America, Secretary: H. Richard Pascoe, 785 Valley View Road, Fornay, TX 75126.

BREEDERS

Your dog's breeder is the first and *most important* professional that you will encounter. If you choose your breeder with care, he or she can point you in the direction of the rest of the professionals you will need for support. A good breeder is such an important resource for you because dedicated, ethical and professional breeders know the strengths and weaknesses of their breed. They study to understand the potential medical problems and the dietary needs of their breed as well.

Breeders are usually aware of the most qualified trainers, veterinarians and boarding kennels in their area.

WHAT IS A REPUTABLE BREEDER?

Reputable breeders are people who stand behind their puppies with a written contract, the quality of the puppies being first priority.

Remember that when you are looking for a reputable and knowledgeable breeder, working quality must be a priority because of the fact that you will be looking for a dog with the right temperament and working drive for business security. This means that while breed championships are a plus, working quality such as European sport titles or police, security or personal protection training evident in the parents' backgrounds are your top priority. Optimally, you should be able to see the puppy's parents work. Videotape has made it possible to view a dog working without having to arrange a command performance.

A good breeder whelps the puppies indoors and looks after their well-being with proper diet and medical care, i.e., shots, worming and so on. Pups should be kept as clean as possible and should be raised on a surface that is easy to clean (not dirt), such as cement, Astroturf or linoleum.

A good breeder will have all of the health requirements and certifications, such as OFA (Orthopedic Foundation for Animals) and eye certifications (CERF), as well as any other health checks required for your breed. Good breeders always have goals in mind for their breeding program. Improving temperament, anatomy, or breed characteristics are all suitable goals, as well as a general concept of the ideal (working) specimen.

How to Find a Reputable Breeder

Once you have decided on a breed, there are several ways to find a reputable breeder.

1. Call your local breed club. You can get the number to the club in your area by calling the local dog show superintendent.
2. Attend a local dog show or Schutzhund Trial and speak to people who own the breed you are looking for about breeders and clubs in your area.
3. Speak with dog trainers in your area regarding breeders whom they would recommend.
4. Ask your veterinarian if he/she can recommend a reputable breeder.

You may speak to a dozen people before you locate a reputable breeder. Don't go with the first person you hear about; even among top breeders, there are some who have more to offer than others. The best advice is, **"Take your time and do your homework!"**

TEMPERAMENT TESTING PUPPIES

Even eight-week-old puppies can be tested for things like noise shyness, pain threshold, nervousness, dominance, prey drive and, to a small degree, defense.

Nervousness and Stress Level Tests

Key Test

With all the puppies loose in an approximately 10 foot by 10 foot area, take your keys out and call the puppies, shaking the keys. Now throw the keys down in the middle of the puppies. Note their reactions. You do not want to see them cower and run. You want to see the pups stop, orient toward the noise and then go investigate it. The pup that picks up the keys and runs away with them is dominant and assertive.

Key Test—The puppy should investigate the jingle of the keys when they are shaken and dropped to the ground.

The most dominant puppy runs away with the keys.

Mechanical Toy Test—Curiosity is displayed by these Boxer puppies who readily pounce on the mechanical toy.

Noise Shyness—Banging two pans to-gether is a good test for noise shyness. This puppy cocks his head to the side and displays steady nerves.

Hold Down—A puppy that is dominant by nature will not be comfortable being held on its back. The puppy should struggle to remain upright.

Mechanical Toy Test

Take a mechanical toy (something that walks, bounces, barks, etc.) and turn it on in the center of the room where the puppies are playing. Again, you want to see the puppies stop and look and then investigate. If they bark at it, this is a good sign of puppy defensiveness, but it is even better if they touch it. The pup that investigates and plays with the toy is assertive and dominant.

Elevation Test

Put the puppy on a table or raised counter where the surface is not slippery, but where the pup can see over the edge. This will ensure that the reaction you see is caused by the elevation and not the slippery surface. If the pup cowers down and shakes, you will note nervousness. If the pup wags its tail and looks ready to jump, the opposite is obviously true of this pup. Do *not* let the pup jump.

Pain Threshold

Take the pup's foot in your hand and, very lightly, pinch the webbing between the toes. You want to see the puppy notice the pinch and pull away gently or lightly put its mouth over your hand indicating it doesn't care for what you are doing.

If the pup does not seem to even notice, you will need to keep a watch on whether this puppy is too dull or lacking in drives and awareness. On the other hand, if you see the puppy panic and yelp or bite at your hand aggressively and thrash about, you will need to worry about low pain threshold, poor nerves and, ultimately, a fear-biter.

Noise Shyness

Take two or three small stainless steel pans into the puppy room. At a distance of six to eight feet from the puppies, drop the pans to the ground one at a time.

Note the puppies' responses. They should freeze, orient themselves to the noise and then choose to investigate or ignore, but they should not shy and hide.

Prey Drive—Prey Drive can be observed at a young age, as with these Boxer pups and a stuffed tug toy.

It is entirely possible to have an unlikely breed show the right amounts of drive for the work. This Dalmatian is high in Defense Drive and trained in Level 1 protection.

DOMINANCE TEST

Hold Down

Take each puppy and in turn flip them over on their backs. Hold your hand over their shoulders, just below the neck, as if you were pinning the shoulders down. Hold the pup in this position as long as you can. Does the pup tolerate and then struggle to get loose? Does the pup freeze? Does the pup panic and bite at you? Does the pup alternately struggle, settle, struggle, settle? To a degree, the more struggling the pup does, the more dominant the pup is likely to be. A dominant pup does not like to be pinned down, as this is a dominant act from the pup's point of view.

If the pup goes wild and bites at you, be aware that this may be a future stress case and fear-biter.

PREY DRIVE

Balls, Rags, Pup Tugs

Drag a pup tug or rag in front of the pups. You will want to see the pups chase and bite at it. Chasing but using the paws to pin the tug is not as good because it shows a tendency for weak biting in the future.

Observing the Litter

Try to test and observe the litter *three* times before you select. This helps to ensure that your observation of the pups is correct. Pups, like humans, have off days. A pup who just woke up, just finished eating or feels ill may not display a true temperament. Try to test puppies before they eat.

The breeder should be an excellent resource if you know what questions to ask. Ask questions such as: Who dominates the food dish? Who dominates a new toy? Who barks and growls when startled? Who runs forward to investigate a stranger? Who dominates in play? *See if your observations match the breeder's.*

Good breeders will put identifying collars, ribbons or drops of paint on each pup in order to color-code them. This is done so that such observations as health and temperament can be noted.

Good Luck!

CHAPTER VI

YOUR RELATIONSHIP WITH
YOUR K-9

If it is your desire to have an exceptional K-9, you will need to have an exceptional relationship with your K-9. Any dog who has ever amazed you with his/her working ability has a good handler and trainer who has dedicated many hours to training. It is not only training that makes the difference. It is the relationship—the love, the trust, the mutual reliance—that is the cement that bonds the handler/K-9 team.

BUYING AN ADULT

The decision to purchase an adult dog for business security should be taken seriously. There are pros and cons to buying an adult.

PROS

1. Immediate protection for people in immediate danger.
2. There is no puppy stage to go through and you do not have to go through months of training over a two-year period.

---

3. For people with physical disabilities, the unruly adolescent stage has passed.

4. The health and soundness of the dog are, for the most part, obvious and an entire physical exam is possible.

5. Avoid the disappointment of finding out the puppy doesn't have the proper traits for the work.

6. You can pay the same amount for an already trained adult ($3,500–$6,100, general prices as of this writing) and have an immediate result, as opposed to a puppy whose care and training over a two-to-three-year period will cost approximately $3,500 (including purchase price, training and veterinary care).

CONS

1. You will not have the bonding in the most impressionable period of the puppy's life: birth to age six months.

2. You do not have the ability to form behavior—such as getting along with children, cats or livestock—with an adult. What you get is determined by the dog's past, which is sometimes unknown.

3. If you have young children, the dog may not be trustworthy with them. Puppies are recommended for couples with young children.

4. You are saddled with the dog's baggage from previous relationships. This means any learned fears or prejudices are carried with the dog for life.

5. You must have reliable support people to help you determine if the dog is a good investment. There are imported dogs being sold with falsified papers. Falsified Schutzhund titles are common. The best way to determine if the titles are fraudulent is to have a knowledgeable trainer test the dog. If the dog is supposed to be a Schutzhund II and does not know how to do a bark and hold or retrieve over a high jump, you will know something is wrong. Health problems are common. A good veterinarian should do a total health check.

It is recommended that you start with a puppy and socialize the puppy with children if the dog will live with or encounter children.

THE BONDING PROCESS

The bonding process with an adult dog takes time. We use a timetable of three days, three weeks and three months. It takes three days for a dog to adjust to being in a new environment. It takes three weeks for the dog to begin to form a relationship with you and trust you. It takes three months for the dog to feel like you are the owner.

The easiest way to a dog's heart is through the stomach. The dog depends on people for food. This is a fact of life that the dog learns from puppyhood. If it is your desire to have an exceptional relationship with your dog, you must feed the dog yourself. Going for walks and playing ball with the new dog are good ideas, but don't put pressure on the dog to release the ball or do perfect Obedience for you before you have built a relationship.

Every dog is different with regard to the time it takes to bond. A rule of thumb is the higher the dog's security prone temperament, the longer it takes to bond. It is imperative that the dog trusts you, due to the fact that you are to work together as a *security team.* This relationship has to be solid, like a police officer and K-9. When in a real situation, trust is of the utmost importance.

WHO'S THE BOSS?

You had better be the boss if you own a protection dog, especially for business security duties. This is why *it is critical that the handler is trained* to handle the dog properly. Even a well-trained dog put in the hands of a weak or ambivalent handler can be a liability. The dog looks around and decides that nobody is in charge, so the dog takes charge.

As previously mentioned, protection dogs by nature have assertive and dominant personality traits or temperaments, therefore the handler must control the dog like a drill sergeant. The person who is also assertive and has dominant personality traits is a prime candidate to be a good K-9 handler. If, after assessing your own personality, you do not believe that you can be assertive enough for

"Honey! Get the dog training book; I can't remember what to do next!" Who's the boss? You'd better be!

a dog who is a man-stopper, you may want to step down to a Level 1–type mascot/alarm dog. This dog, by nature, is less dominant and assertive and, therefore, not the potential liability that the temperament of 8 or 9 could be in the wrong hands.

READING THE DOG

A good handler is constantly aware of where the dog is at all times and what the dog is focused on. Awareness is not only a key to security, but also a key to handling a security K-9.

Because dogs do not possess the ability to actually reason, they work primarily on instinct and conditioned response. This is why it is so important for the handler to be aware of the dog's thought processes and foresee what the dog's likely response will be in any given situation. The handler must foresee that through the dog's eyes a crutch may look like a weapon, or a friendly bear hug may look like an assault.

Likewise, the handler has to know the K-9's limitations. Every dog has some kind of weakness. The weakness in a dog can be concealed by the owner, but if found it can be exploited by a criminal. The owner must also read the dog in relation to these weaknesses and train to proof the dog as much as possible, as well as try to conceal the weaknesses from the public. For instance, if the dog has a fear of water or a weakness for pizza, you don't want to announce this to your customers. If you understand the dog's weaknesses, you can both anticipate the dog's responses and avoid conflict.

A good example of this is the case of a police dog who was responding to a burglary at a tire shop. The dog was sent in on a building search. When nothing was heard from the suspect or the dog, the K-9 officer entered the building to find the K-9—a 115-pound Rottweiler—playfully throwing tires up in the air. The K-9 handler had failed to realize that the dog's favorite toy was a tire. In the dog's mind, he had hit the jackpot—like a kid in a toy store.

OWNERSHIP AWARENESS AND RESPONSIBILITIES

Awareness cannot be overemphasized, as it is both the key to security in general and the key to being a good security K-9 handler. An alert and aware handler watches the dog's body language and eye focus. A good handler is also aware of the wind direction and changes in the dog's attitudes and behaviors. The aware K-9 handler is in tune with the dog's health and welfare and realizes that when the dog is ill, rest and recuperation are necessary.

Ownership Responsibility is important and is somewhat akin to the responsibilities of being a parent. The dog cannot speak to you to tell you that something hurts or that it's thirsty or hot. You the owner have to care enough to *tune in.* Your responsibilities do not stop with the dog, but extend to your neighborhood and the patrons of your business.

There is a big problem today with loose dogs. Many people have the misconception that they are being kind to their dogs by letting them run free around the neighborhood. People who do this are really guilty of abuse. Some of these dogs end up as road kills, or maimed by cars or in fights with other animals. In addition, there is the danger people encounter when they swerve to avoid hitting the dog with their car. The loose dog can also knock down a child or elderly person or terrorize them on the street. It is difficult to walk your dog on a leash or ride your horse for fear of a loose dog attacking you. It is the owner's responsibility to keep the dog under control and contained on his/her property. The Obedience trained dog will be easier to contain.

The business security K-9 is a special creature in that this dog *must be well trained and well managed,* because this dog will come into contact with patrons of the business. To be an effective deterrent, the dog must come across as *well trained* and immediately *responsive* to the handler.

BREAK AND PLAYTIME

The business security K-9 needs to have break and playtime built into the daily routine. Taking a break is the same for the dog as it is for humans. A break relieves stress, allows for the dog to relieve itself and allows the dog to stretch, scratch, sniff and do all the things a dog likes to do when not under command. Whether the dog spends the day riding shotgun in an eighteen-wheeler, or lying quietly next to the jeweler, there must be break times built into the schedule.

Playtime, on the other hand, is best reserved for off-time. Dogs are so easily conditioned that if playtime is allowed during work hours, the dog is likely to become overly excited and excessively active. The business dog should be quiet and reserved, but at the same time, *aware.* Playing with the dog will do the opposite. The dog is likely to be anxious, excited and distracted. If you play hard, the dog will come back to the workplace and sleep. A good time to play with the dog is after work. Throwing a ball, playing Frisbee, swimming or bike riding are all good types of play and exercise and take only about twenty minutes. **Do not exercise or play hard with the dog immediately before or after the dog eats. This places the dog at greater risk for bloat and gastric torsion.**

DOG PSYCHOLOGY—THE DOG'S POINT OF VIEW (POV)

To really understand how to properly manage, handle and train each dog to optimum potential, you must be able to put yourself in the dog's place and look at the world through the dog's eyes.

To do this you must imagine yourself with eyesight that lacks the details of depth, image and color. Imagine that you have much better peripheral vision and much better detection of movement—somewhat like looking at the world through an extremely wide angle lens with no attention to detail. Now imagine that you can hear ten times better and with more detail. For example, you can hear a vehicle coming when it's still a mile from your home.

Sit? (English) Sitz? (German) Shév? (Hebrew) Assis? (French) . . . You may train your dog in any language or code, as long as you remain consistent.

Training, conditioning and maturity—a natural progression with regard to all dogs. Training is started with the young pup; conditioning the behavior is long-term and is maintained through the adolescent stage; then the natural maturity of the dog will set the behaviors. Shown are Mikey (3 months), Buck (1) and Barcez (7).

As a dog, your nose is your best asset. You can sense changes in the weather. The wind carries smells to you from miles away and you can remember people and other animals for years based on their smell. You can smell another dog and know where it has been, whether it is ill, what it is has eaten and so on.

Imagine that you cannot understand a thing that people say, other than those words and body language signals that you see repetitively. You balance this weakness with your strength of being able to quickly understand the temperament and personality traits of a new person. Using your instincts and sense of smell, you can quickly determine if a person is assertive, passive or even if someone has a chemical imbalance.

Imagine that you have no reasoning ability. Money has no value to you, in fact, nothing material has any value to you. You may choose to chew on a chair or a stick of wood.

If you were a dog you would have *no concept of right or wrong*. To say dogs knew they did wrong is a false concept. To punish a dog would imply that the dog could understand that the punishment is related to an action that was wrong. This would be giving the dog the credit for human moral values and reasoning ability. The extent of the dog's learning ability is trial and error and conditioned behavior. A dog can understand *correction* that is directly associated with an action. For instance, if the dog is digging and you startle the dog with your voice or a "shake can," the dog will associate the action with the *correction*. This relates to trial and error. Conversely, if the dog soils the carpet and you return home two hours later to punish the dog, this is done in vain, as the dog cannot make the connection between action and consequence.

If you were a dog, social interaction would be very important to you. Dogs are pack animals and therefore have an inherent need to live within a social structure. To the dog, any animal in the home is a member of the pack. Any human in the home is also a member of the pack. Social hierarchy is defined by the limits that the dominant pack member sets for the rest of the pack, as well as where each member of the pack falls in the pecking order. Temperament is directly related to the pecking order, as the more assertive and dominant pack members draw the boundaries of behavior for the less assertive pack members.

WHAT DOES THIS HAVE TO DO WITH YOU?

It means that if you do not set boundaries for your dog's behavior, you may allow your dog to be *alpha,* the most dominant member of your pack. The dog then becomes assertive, perhaps by growling at another member of the pack over food or articles, refusing to obey commands or willfully dominating just by being overwhelming.

A dog who dominates the household is a liability simply because in the dog's mind there is nobody else taking control. This dog has become alpha. If you attempt to train this dog, and you find submission to your will, this dog is what we consider an alpha *candidate.* This means when challenged he/she will step down a peg. The true alpha will never submit.

In a business capacity, it is important that the dog takes a subservient role to you, the handler. This is a necessary aspect of your bonding with the dog if you are to work together as a team.

HOW DO YOU ESTABLISH THE LEADERSHIP/ALPHA ROLE WITH YOUR DOG?

You set parameters for the dog's behavior, giving the dog guidelines to live by such as:

- Stopping at **established boundaries** in the store, house, yard, etc.
- **Establishing places** in the store, house, etc., where the dog is expected to lie down when inside.
- **Establishing basic Obedience** commands on and off leash through a professional trainer.
- **Do not allow the dog to steal** food or articles of clothing.

111

- **Do not allow the dog to lie on the bed or couch.** This puts you on an equal level in the dog's mind.

One very important thing to remember is that in general, *you should not respond to the dog, the dog should respond to you.* For instance, the dog gets in the habit of nudging you for attention and you always give it. Or the dog goes to the pantry and stares, looking to you for a biscuit and you always respond by giving one. These are both examples of you being trained by the dog. To reverse these roles, you simply add one more step to this scenario—tell your dog "No," and do not respond. Then, at a time of your choosing, tell the dog to "Sit" or "Down," then give the attention or the biscuit. You will have established a leadership role with the dog. This is because *you* set the parameters of the dog's behavior, not vice versa.

If you are going to take a leadership (alpha) role with a security K-9, it is important that you are the right type of leader. *You do not want to rule the dog with an iron fist.* If you attempt this you'll destroy your protection dog. You will run the risk that when the bad guy comes around the dog will jump behind you. All this time you've been establishing how much of a bully you can be; *bullies are not effective leaders.*

The best way for a handler to be alpha, but not overdominate the dog, is to work with the dog using *the balance system.*

APPLYING CORRECTION AND PRAISE

The balance system represents the corrections (negative) and praise (positive) that you dish out to your dog. Using the balance system, you attempt to balance every correction (negative) with a positive. The trick is to correct negative behavior and then drop any negative feeling toward the dog. Then create a reason to praise. If the dog corrects the behavior after the mistake, you have good reason to praise. If the dog doesn't correct the behavior, correct appropriately until proper behavior is achieved, then praise lavishly.

- If you overpraise and undercorrect, the dog will be wild.
- If you underpraise and overcorrect, the dog will shut down and be fearful.
- If you keep your praise and correction balanced, the dog will be balanced and under control.

Correction has to be handled in a manner the dog can relate to. When we study the actions of a bitch with puppies, we see that she will both startle them and grab them by the scruff of the neck. We can use the scruff of the neck routine with a young pup to a certain degree, but it is the startle reflex that we use throughout the dog's training. Correction can be applied in the following ways:

1. Startle the dog with a quick motion, loud noise or water. Any of these will cause a small adrenaline rush in the dog.
2. Use a loud and low tone of voice when you correct the dog, as tone of voice is critical.
3. Use bad feel, taste, noise and smell to correct the dog using the dog's instincts and senses.
4. Using a German steel training collar, give the dog a quick jerk and release on the collar at the same time as the "No" is issued. This uses both the sense of feel and the startle reaction, if done properly.

Praise is the dog's paycheck. It is what the dog works for, so it is critical. Praise should be given in the following manner:

1. High pitched tone of voice used to "cheerlead" the dog through the commands. Voice should give support and encouragement and motivation.
2. Physical petting or soothing as required, ranging from excited pats to soothing strokes down the back or an affectionate scratch on the chest.
3. Rewards in the form of hotdog pieces, chicken nuggets, liver, etc., or the dog's jute tug or ball can be given when appropriate.

VERBAL SKILLS AND FOREIGN LANGUAGES

Dogs relate to each other in tones. Low and sharp tones relate to corrective, assertive behavior. This is why our corrections to the dog should also be in a low but sharp tone. On the other hand, praise is high pitched and more drawn out, like a high-pitched whine. This is the way the dog greets or shows extreme excitement.

Humans relate in much the same manner, subconsciously. So it is not difficult at all for us to adapt to this type of communication with the dog. Commands should be kept to one syllable and should sound distinctly different from each other.

A dog can be trained in any language as long as commands can be found that are easy for the dog to identify. This means the commands should be short and easy to separate. Since the dog doesn't know anything about language, you can literally pick any word you want for each command. It is perfectly acceptable to teach the dog five commands in five different languages. It makes no difference to the dog.

One reason that many people like to train in different languages or a code all of their own is so that strangers cannot command the dog. This is definitely a plus, and it should be understood that a stranger cannot use your dog against you or override your dog in any case if your training is complete.

TRAINING, CONDITIONING AND MATURITY

This is probably the biggest "pothole" in the road to completing your goals with your dog. It really all boils down to one thing: *your patience.* Many people set goals that they never reach simply because they lose patience along the way and drop the project. The dog is a living creature and lives with you. The dog cannot be cast aside as easily as an exercise bicycle.

When you consider having a K-9 for security purposes and raising it from a puppy, you will go through ups and downs and a lot of training for two or three years. The reality of raising a security

Backing up the Dog—This staged situation setup illustrates how the tables can be turned on the perpetrator if the business owner is prepared.

puppy is that regardless of the puppy or who the trainer is, your puppy will have a particular set of strengths and weaknesses, and will go through the three stages of mental, physical and emotional growth as all dogs do. Each dog matures at a slightly different pace. Every dog owner-in-training needs to understand that dog training is a fairly short-term process in the sense that a dog can learn all basic five commands in a period of weeks. *Conditioning takes months,* and maturity setting in takes years—somewhat like children. At least we're only talking three years in this case. A rule of thumb to work by is:

- Training command(s)   3 weeks
- Conditioning to set in   3 months
- Maturity to set in   3 years

} *In* no way *does this imply that any of these stages is* complete *in this period of time.*

A big downfall for people comes right in the middle of training. When the dog is approximately two years of age, the owner may begin to doubt the dog's abilities, and may feel that either the training or the dog is not proceeding fast enough. This is somewhat like the runner who "hits the wall." The good runners keep going and break through to get a second wind and finish the race. There will be some dog trainers who will hit the wall and give up.

In training, most people start out excited about the prospect of what the end result will be; they tend to be very idealistic. Training begins as expected with a young puppy—ups and downs—but *it's a puppy.* The problem with patience typically begins when the puppy no longer looks like a puppy—in adolescence. Adolescence is the longest period of puppyhood. It starts at about eight months of age and continues until the dog is two and sometimes up to three years of age.

Through this entire time period, the dog should be in various stages of training and be receiving consistent conditioning on all previous areas taught. This is the most tedious and repetitive part of the training process and it is easy for people to lose patience and feel that the dog should be progressing faster. The one factor that neither the trainer nor the handler can dictate is the dog's maturity rate. Dogs are all individuals and, like people, they grow in physical, mental and emotional rates that are very individual.

THE REAL STUFF

Dogs should not start serious protection training until one year of age. For most dogs, this is the time when the hormones are kicking in and the dog is experimenting with aggression anyway. If the dog is being trained on an ongoing basis, in an established program, you would say that the average dog could complete its security training for business security at three years of age. For personal protection, two to three years of age.

As previously stated, from age eighteen months to two years typically, in the learning phases of protection, people often lose patience. They are seeing a dog as an adult because of physical size, but who is actually still very much an adolescent *inside*. At this age, they are in a very up and down learning stage where they will seem proficient at the work one day and lackluster the next. This is all a part of training. When any of us learn, we go through good and bad days with the skill we are learning. So do dogs. Our advice to owners is *stick with the program*.

SETTING GOALS AND MAKING CHOICES

When you have a K-9 in mind as part of your security plan, by now you should have decided whether to start with a trained adult or a puppy. Next, you will need to establish goals for the dog. This is important to do *before* you choose the dog or puppy because it is critical to get the right temperament for your needs. Review Chapter IV, The Right K-9 Temperament for Your Needs.

A true assessment of your threat level is needed as well as an understanding of what the temperament of your prospective puppy

Very young puppies can start training with food as a motivator. Simply hold the food in the direction you wish the puppy to go. Use the appropriate command with the action. Later, you may eliminate food altogether or use it occasionally as a motivator.

Stand; hold in front of nose

Heel; hold just in front of nose and walk

Sit; hold above head so puppy has to tilt head back

Facing pup, hold food in front of nose and move backward

Hold the food down near the pup's front paws

or dog should be. You should discuss this issue, especially in the case of a husband and wife running a business together. In many cases the husband and wife do not agree on the desired temperament. It is not unusual to have one person say, "We want kind of a mild one because we mainly want a pet." Yet the other person will say, "Do you think the puppy will be able to go all the way in protection?" Then they decide on a mild puppy, and months later when the dog is eighteen months old and coming along slowly in protection training, one of them will be impatient with the dog's progress and will want to see the dog acting highly defensive to strangers. This is a problem when the desires of the partners are at two opposite ends of the spectrum.

In the case that you end up with a puppy or dog who lacks the abilities necessary to do what you desire, you will have to make a difficult decision. Do you follow your goal and get another dog who will suit your purpose? Or will you choose to train the current dog to Level 1 protection and use this dog as an alarm/deterrent (if possible)?

Many times, by accepting the dog's limitations and simply working consistently with the dog's strengths, you will get out-standing results. This was the case with a dog that we trained to be an alarm/deterrent. She was a small Rottweiler bitch and not very high on the protection temperament scale—maybe $7–7^{1}/_{2}$—but she could really act the part by jumping up and down and snarling. Her owner accepted the fact that she was never going to be able to practice apprehension work because she had no desire for physical contact, but she could alarm and deter well. One night the dog caught some youths hiding in her owner's house. She scared them into a laundry room and stood guard by the door until the police came. This dog would not have been likely to even nip these youths, but they didn't know it. There is validity in training for Level 1 even if your dog can go no further (see Chapter IX).

Set your goals and do your best to meet them. If you are advised by your trainer to stop because the dog cannot progress any further,

It is important to teach the dog to look at you when Heeling. Positive reinforcement with the voice helps to keep the dog working happy.

In teaching the dog to Sit when you come to a stop, make sure you roll the dog's hips backward so as not to hurt the dog's back or hips.

you will have to make the decision regarding another dog. However, if the trainer advises you that the dog can progress with time, consistency and maturity, *stick with it.* It will be worth it.

HANDLER AWARENESS AND TRAINING

The dog handler needs as much, if not more, training than the dog. As the handler, it is your responsibility to reason for the team. You must be alert to danger, aware of your K-9 and the K-9's focus, and aware of dangers to your K-9 and the K-9's needs. You also have to be trained to work the dog and back up the dog.

To be a good K-9 handler, you must be in tune with the K-9. You should have a backup plan for action, in the event that something happens that involves the need to help the dog with an apprehension or in defending yourselves.

The dog's job is to buy you enough time to respond with force of your own. How you choose to defend yourself is up to you. Do not stand by and wait for someone else to jump in and save you. It is important for you to think ahead.

CHAPTER VII

OBEDIENCE TRAINING AND
OFFICE MANNERS

OBEDIENCE COMMANDS—LEVEL 1 (FOUR TO SIX MONTHS)

Obedience begins with five basic commands: Heel, Sit, Stay, Come and Down. These commands are the basic foundation of training that any dog should know. After teaching the basics, it is desirable to go on with more advanced training such as retrieving, jumping, scent tests, Sit in motion, Down in motion, Down on Recall and so on. You can accomplish this as all Obedience stems from the five basic commands.

EQUIPMENT

- 6-foot leather or nylon leash
- 30-foot-long line
- 10-inch tab
- Small-link German steel choke chain
- Optional: pinch collar (with older, stronger, assertive dogs)

Collars and leashes should always be purchased with the size and strength of the dog in mind. A large protection dog should be worked on a 1-inch-wide leash, preferably with a brass clip.

Choke chains must be put on correctly to work properly. We recommend small-link choke chains because they release easier than the large oblong links. With the dog on your left-hand side at the Heel position, the chain should come over the top of the neck and down through the O ring. If you hold the ring in your hand, you should be holding the end of the letter P.

FIVE COMMANDS—6-FOOT LEASH

Heel

Teaching Heel will be much easier if the dog is already leash-broken. Start with the dog on your left side and hold the leash across your body in your right hand. Your left hand should be loosely holding the leash over the top.

Start by patting your leg and stepping off with your left foot. Command "Baron, Heel." Begin to encourage with "Good, that-a-baby!" If the dog pulls or barks, give him a quick jerk as a correction with a "No." Keep walking and encouraging.

Make about-turns to maintain attention and tell Baron that he is going with you. When you stop, pull up with your right hand and push down carefully on the dog's rear end, saying "Sit." Praise, once the dog is in this position. The easiest way to teach your dog that the idea is to stay with you in this particular position is to walk quickly to keep the dog's attention. If your dog's head is not up and his eyes are not looking at you, the most likely problem has to do with your intensity, both verbal and physical. When the dog is learning, you should be talking constantly, letting the dog know what is right or wrong.

If you run into problems, try to motivate the dog with food or a toy. Take it a little at a time—three or four steps—before stopping to praise.

Sit

There are three different versions of the Sit command that the dog need to know:

Step 1

1. Sit when told to, regardless of position
2. Sit in front (on Recall)
3. Automatic Sit at the Heel command

By now, you should have already taught the meaning of Sit by using food (Chapter VI). Transfer this to a little game using a toy. After you know that the dog understands the concept, you can move to polish the performance.

Step 2

Polishing the performance means adding correction to your training. By now, your dog knows to plant his/her rear end on the ground when you command "Sit."

The next step would be to correct with "No," and a sharp jerk on the training collar if the dog doesn't follow through. When your dog comes to you, there should be an automatic Sit in front of you. On the Heel command, the dog should sit automatically when you stop. If not, just apply the correction with a "No."

Step 3

Now that the command is understood and the dog knows that you will give a correction, you can begin to use the toy less and less. The toy is a motivator; however, you do not want the dog to become dependent on it. Hopefully, you have developed such a good relationship at this point that your puppy will work just as cheerfully for praise.

Down

The Down command tends to be the most difficult of all because in the dog's mind it is a submissive command. *The older the dog is*

When teaching the Down, you will want to first give the command and show the dog the hand signal. . .

and then help the dog into position enough times to aid the dog in making the connection.

when you begin to teach this command, the harder it will be to teach. This is especially true when you are working the high-stress-level protection candidate. It is best to start with an eight-week-old puppy with food-reward conditioning. If you have not done this, begin with the older pup using food (described in Chapter VI).

When you progress to the toy, there is only one way to use reward properly. Once on the Down, give the dog the toy as a reward for the Down and leave your dog on a Stay with the toy.

For some dogs, this allows you to lengthen the Stay because the dog is comfortable holding or chewing on the toy. For other dogs that become active with the toy and scoot across the ground, you will have to eliminate the toy altogether.

Stay

Stay was not worked on during puppy training because of the dog's short attention span. Even though the pup has matured to the point of being able to learn the Stay command, we still need to realize that four to six months of age is not mature enough to hold this position for a long period of time. We need to ensure short-term successes now, in order to build up to longer periods in the future.

Start with the pup at the Heel position. Give the desired command to Sit or Down. Do not use the toy or food on this command, as your dog will be motivated to come toward you. Signal a Stay, holding the palm of your left hand firmly in front of the dog's nose.

1. Step out in front of the dog (about 2 to 3 feet).
2. Begin to walk slowly in a half circle around your dog, right foot first.
3. Use soothing praise and frequently show the hand signal.

Be ready to step in and correct quickly if the dog starts to move.

After the puppy understands the meaning of the command you may correct with a "No!" and a jerk on the leash using your foot in a downward position. This is done only after the command is issued *and* the puppy refuses.

Leave the dog on a Sit/Stay, showing the palm of your hand often at first as you walk back and forth in a half-circle in front of the pup. **Always praise** when the puppy does well.

Correct the puppy for leaving a Sit/Stay by pulling up and backward on the leash.

Sit/Stay

1. Correct with the leash in an upward manner for a Sit/Stay. Quickly place your dog back in the original spot.
2. Give the signal with your palm up, again.
3. Again, step out and begin your half circle.

Down/Stay

1. For the Down/Stay, step in and step on the leash as the dog is getting up. This will anchor the dog to the spot.
2. Reach for the leash above where it is anchored.
3. Correct the dog in a downward manner.
4. Once the dog is down, give the signal for Stay by showing the palm of your hand.
5. Step back out again and begin your half circle.

Anchoring the Dog

If you have a particularly difficult time with the dog moving toward you on the Stay, you may want to "anchor" for a while until the dog gets the idea. You can anchor by using a tree or post of some sort. Using a 30-foot-long line, wrap it around the post or tree and connect the other end to your dog's collar. The line should go around the post at the same level the collar is on the dog. Thus, if this is the Sit/Stay, the line will be between 2 to 3 feet from the ground.

On the Down/Stay, the line will be under the dog at ground level. To the dog, you will still seem to be controlling the leash. If the dog tries to move toward you, it will be impossible. Your dog will be automatically corrected with any momentum when coming to you.

Recall (Come)

The Recall or Come command should be introduced during free movement. Do not call a dog from a stay position at this point. If this mistake is made, it will take much longer to correct breaking.

We want to emphasize the Come command. This is because it is a key to protecting yourself from excessive liability as well as assuring the dog's safety. The food and toy rewards work well here because they motivate the dog to come quickly.

In AKC and Schutzhund competition, the dog must come and sit front. Upon command the dog will then proceed to the Heel position to finish the exercise. In French and Dutch sports, the dog immediately proceeds to the Heel position. This is the manner in which we prefer to train personal protection dogs if they are not going to compete in AKC trials or Schutzhund events. Beyond this difference, the command is basically taught the same way.

Example:

1. The dog is wandering and sniffing around, not on any command. The release word "Okay" should have been given.
2. If you have been using food in the puppy stage, your dog will already associate coming to you with reward. If not, begin with food. Call the dog to you and wave a toy.
3. As your dog comes to you, teach the dog properly to:

- Sit in front—hold the toy (or food) in front of you. Say "Sit" and after your dog has been sitting for five or six seconds, give the toy and praise.
- Sit at Heel—as the dog comes to you, step back and bring the toy in front of the dog's nose, with the dog following the toy around behind your back. Bring the toy up as your dog comes into the Heel position and say "Sit." Wait five or six seconds. Give the toy and *praise*!

After your dog has learned to follow the toy, you can move on to the next step, keeping the toy on you (in your belt or pocket). Call the dog to you and into the proper position for the Sit. If the dog does not follow through, use a leash correction. Once the dog has complied, give the toy as a reward.

Be sure you are patient and do not go too quickly through these steps. Depending on the age of the dog you are training, each step can span a period of days or weeks.

Walk backward as you call the dog to come. This will keep the pup interested and moving quickly.

Encourage the dog to sit close and look up at you. The dog should not touch you.

PAIRING YOUR EXERCISES

Training will go much smoother if you pair exercises that complement one another. For example, the first lesson taught could be walking at the Heel position and Come when called. They are of the same concept—staying near the handler and sitting when the dog stops. These commands are much easier to learn together than the concepts of Stay and Come.

Sit and Down can be paired together as they are also similar commands. Stay should be taught separately after the Sit and Down are well established. There are many other Obedience commands that can and should be taught, such as:

- Stand for Examination
- Figure eight
- Down on Recall
- Stay on Recall
- Retrieve over High Jump
- Sit in motion
- Stand in motion
- Down in motion
- Food refusal
- Scent Discrimination
- Change of positions at a distance
- Broad Jump
- Stay with handler out of sight
- Obstacle work
- Directed Retrieves
- Send away

Since this book is based on the business security K-9, we will only explain those that can be applied directly to this work.

30-FOOT-LONG LINE WORK

After the five basic Obedience commands have been covered and you are happy with the dog's performance on the 6-foot leash, you

The Send-away involves teaching a dog to run straight away from you on command.

The 30-foot-long line allows you to practice Sit and Down/Stays at a distance and still maintain control of the dog.

Toss the extra line out to the side as you reel the dog in.

Passing a toy or food reward behind your back will help the pup learn to Finish properly at the Heel position.

As the dog comes around on the Finish, direct her to your left Heel position by stepping forward and patting your left thigh.

are ready to proceed to the long line. The long line is used to establish your control at a distance while at the same time allowing the dog more freedom. This is not a new concept. You most likely have used this piece of equipment to give your puppy break-time before this point. You have probably called your dog a few times using this as well.

You will now use this piece of equipment to build up your distance work. Your goal will be to make the long line as insignificant as possible in the *dog's eyes*. In reality, it is a very significant piece of equipment to you as it allows you to have control of the dog's actions from a distance.

HEEL

Begin by putting the bulk of the line in your right hand. This is away from the dog's line of vision on your left. Drop the line behind your back and over your right shoulder only. Now it is out of sight even on your left.

Keep your left hand swinging free as you do your Heeling exercise, and make turns often. Try to use only your voice for correction and encouragement. If the dog gets way out of line, reach back to the line and give a quick jerk. Show the dog, *if* need be, that you still have the ability to correct.

TURNS

Practice a lot of squared turns to the left and right using this procedure. If the dog tends to lead, make more frequent left and about-turns in order to check the pace. If necessary, jerk just as you make the turn, to keep your dog alert.

The slow dog will need about-turns and right turns to keep up. Instead of applying the correction into the turn, you will apply motivation and encouragement in the form of your voice and a toy.

RECALL (COME) COMMAND

The Recall command will now involve more distractions (i.e., someone talking, offering food or a toy, etc.).

Step 1

Call the dog away and give the chance to respond. Give a "No" command and jerk if you do not get a response. Praise the dog into the proper position. Praise only after a complete Sit at the Heel position has been achieved.

Step 2

You now want to reach a point with the dog where the line is not so obvious. To do this, leave the line on the ground and call, using only your voice; however, reward if it is necessary for encouragement. Additionally, pick up the line only to make the correction. Try not to rely on the line, as it will not be there later on. Work through Sit and Down/Stay on the long line before going to Step 3.

Step 3

You have completed both the Sit and Down/Stay on the long line and Step 2 of Recall before going to this step.

RECALL FROM THE STAY

Put the dog on a Sit/Stay and move to the end of the line. Call the dog to come after about a minute. Give a gentle tug and encouragement, showing your approval.

From this point, finish your exercise with praise and reward. Recall from the Down/Stay is the same. We suggest you do this second, as it is easier to pull a dog from a Sit than from a Down.

SIT AND DOWN/STAY

With the help of your long line, you can begin to teach the dog the Stay at a distance with more distractions. Work your way slowly away from the dog until you are accomplishing Sit and Down/Stays at 30 feet.

DISTRACTIONS

Distractions are very important at this juncture of training. Do not go crazy throwing everything but the kitchen sink at the dog. Give one test at a time. Always be ready to correct when providing distractions.

Go to the dog and always give a quick jerk with your correction, saying "No." If you do not jerk, correction will quickly lose its meaning. Possible distractions include other dogs, people, toys, noises, etc.

OBEDIENCE COMMANDS—LEVEL 2 (SIX TO TWELVE MONTHS): OFF-LEASH OBEDIENCE

You are ready to work towards off-leash control when you find yourself *rarely* having to correct the dog with the leash.

LIGHT LEASH

The first step will be to use a very light leash, one that is not much heavier than a parachute cord, or the type you should use on a Toy breed. With small dogs, we use dental floss. With large protection breeds, we use a Toy breed leash.

Drop the leash and proceed through your commands as if the leash weren't there. It is there for you to step on in order to anchor the dog. Do not step on it by accident. This can set back your training. Keep your motivation high at this stage of your training. Read your dog to know if you need to use voice, a toy or food for motivation. By this stage, it is preferable that the dog is voice motivated. If your dog needs more motivation, do not hesitate to use it.

TAB

Next you will use the handle or the tab, a short piece of leash or handle loop no more than 10 inches in length. This allows you to correct when necessary, while at the same time having the dog off of the leash. You need the tab because a quick, solid correction must be an option during this phase of training. Reaching down to find the O ring of the collar can be both time-consuming and painful.

Hiding the owner out of sight, the dog on a Down/Stay can be tested with distractions such as a ball rolling by . . .

or a stranger offering food.

Run through all five commands on the tab. Do this in a safe place where your dog cannot escape or get hit by a car. Remember to use whatever motivation is necessary.

Start working the dog close to you and progress to a comfortable distance from the dog. Always remember that you are free to go back to any of the previous steps. Just because the dog can now work off-leash does *not* mean that you will never again use a leash. The same goes for the long line and the light line. The law demands the use of a leash in public places for everyone's safety. It is also good practice for the dog. The long line allows you to keep a distance and at the same time exercise safety. Practice your doors and boundaries with the long line, light line and tab as well. The light line and the tab should be used for the Place command.

The difficulty in getting the dog successfully off-leash will depend on a number of factors. In general, the younger the dog when you began conditioning, the easier it will be to work off-leash.

THE COLLAR-WISE DOG

Dogs usually become collar-wise (meaning that they obey only when the collar is on). We usually put the collar on for training and then take it off when we are finished so that the dog will not accidentally choke in the kennel or elsewhere.

The problem here is that the dog thinks, "There's no collar on me so that means I don't have to work." To break this cycle, we must first leave the collar *on* 100 percent of the time for at least a two-month period. This period will include the time when we are teaching the advanced work. We must minimize the dangers by eliminating everything we can find that the dog may get hung up on. This is especially true when the dog is in the crate while we are away.

Note the tab hanging between the dog's front legs. This allows the handler the ability to correct the dog without fumbling around for the collar.

Using a very lightweight leash, you can begin to work toward your off-leash training by letting the dog drag the leash.

OFFICE AND HOME MANNERS—BOUNDARY CONTROL, DOOR CRASHING, PLACE COMMAND

Office and home manners are defined as the limits that you set for the dog or puppy in your office and home environment. There are three standard office and home manners:

Boundary control: Teaching the pup to stay within set boundary limits in the office, house or yard. Teaching the pup not to go into the street unless you say "Okay." These are safety rules.

Door Crashing: Another safety rule it teaching the pup not to go in or out of doors or gates unless you say "Okay."

Place Command: Teaching the pup to lie down in a specific place in the office or house. There are typically one to three places that are "his" or "hers" in the office or house. This command will work well for your protection later.

BOUNDARY CONTROL—FOUR MONTHS

First, you need to decide where you want your boundaries to be. In most offices and homes, we recommend starting with curbs leading into the street. Next, we move to the sidewalk boundaries leading to the neighboring yards or offices. Many times these boundaries are not clearly marked. Temporarily use a garden hose or a board across this area until the dog is conditioned. Some people would rather have the dog stop at the sidewalk (or in the case of a condominium complex, the boundary may be at a garage door).

This is a simple procedure. First, walk the pup along the

By the time the dog is working off leash the commands should be carried out swiftly and with a positive attitude . . .

If the speed or attitude is not evident, you will need to go back to your long line.

A dog who is expected to protect the owner must be confident. An Agility course helps to build confidence.

boundary that you have chosen. Use a 6-foot leash and a standard choke/slip–type training collar. Bring the dog to the curb and slowly step into the street. If the pup attempts to follow you, give a quick jerk-and-release on the collar and say "No!" Praise as the dog backs up. You must correct quickly when the dog steps into the street. Your "No" must project the urgency you would feel if the pup were about to be struck by a car. Praise must be sincere and exuberant when your dog returns to the curb.

After you practice on curbs for several days, proceed with sidewalk boundaries. These boundaries are less obvious. It will be necessary to place something across the sidewalk so that the pup will easily notice it. Practice stopping at this point.

THE RELEASE WORD: "OKAY"

After your dog has learned to stop at the correct boundaries, what if you want to go for a walk and your pup refuses to leave the yard? Now you can teach the release work—"Okay." Do not overdo this. You do not want to undo the conditioning that you have started. You will want to do this in conjunction with Obedience training so that you can say, "Okay, Buck, Heel." This way, the dog understands that this is Obedience when you allow a release. It is not a release that allows the dog to run down the street. When you give the "Okay," gently pull the pup toward you and praise. Command "Heel" and walk off with Buck in the Heel position at your left side. Praise as you walk and keep your pup's spirit up.

The next step in boundary work is to add distance and distractions. Advance to a 30-foot-long line. Let it drag on the ground as you walk the dog toward the street. Never use a command when you are working boundary control, except after you have released with an "Okay." Talk to your pup as you might when you are relaxed: "Buck, want to play?" or "Let's go." If Buck forgets and walks into the street, quickly turn and say "No!" If you need to, pick up the long line and use it to correct. Do this several times in different areas of the boundary.

Next, bring out a ball or a toy. Bounce it in the street. Have children tempt your dog, try food—*anything* the dog could possibly encounter. Be consistent with your corrections. Do this on a regular basis until the dog is six months old and you should be ready to finish the process off-leash.

BOUNDARY CONTROL—SIX MONTHS

Using only a short leash (see Level 2 Obedience), review the same procedure you have been practicing for the last eight weeks. First, try this with the dog next to you, then gradually add distractions and distance. Know how trustworthy your dog is. Use extreme caution if you are located on or near a busy street.

DOOR CRASHING—FOUR MONTHS

The term "door crashing" can be misleading. Door crashing involves teaching the dog not to crash through doors or gates. We handle this in almost the same way as boundary control except for the fact that door crashing is taught both in and out. There are many reasons for this training. The two most common are:

1. To keep the dog from escaping from the office, house or yard.
2. To keep the dog from knocking you over as you go in or out of your doors or gates.

Again, this is not difficult to do, but requires consistency and repetition. Bring the pup to the doorway on the leash. Walk through, but correct if the pup tries to walk through. Give a quick jerk backward with a firm "No!" Praise while the dog stays there. It is this simple to show what you want. Talk, but do not let your pup come to you until you say the magic word—"Okay." Once you release, you can praise and pet the dog. Next, turn around and do the same thing coming the other way.

After you have the pup conditioned to wait until you (and anyone else) walk through the door *before* you release, you can begin something more difficult. Use strangers as distractions to try to cause a mistake. The pup quickly will learn to not be tricked and to make the proper choice by following what the handler indicated. Position should be maintained behind the door or gate, regardless of the temptations of food, children, toys, cats and so on.

DOOR CRASHING—SIX MONTHS

After practicing for eight weeks, you should be able to enforce the same rules using *only* the tab. The pup should now be able to go from place to place in the office or house and yard without a leash.

PLACE COMMAND

The place command provides the following benefits to you and your dog:

1. Allows you and your dog to spend more time together. The dog can even be with you when you are doing daily chores you might otherwise do alone.
2. Allows 90 percent of dog hair and dirt to be in one location for quick and easy cleanup.
3. Allows the family to compromise if one family member doesn't want the dog in the house and others do. The dog's place can be just inside a door on a tile entry surface.
4. The dog can only protect you when *with* you. This command will maximize the time you can spend together.

PLACE COMMAND—FOUR MONTHS

Your pup should be accustomed to coming into the office or house in the crate by now. To effectively teach the Place command, the pup must already understand basic Obedience. It is essential for the dog to comprehend the Down and Stay commands to master the Place command.

Bring the pup into the office or house on a leash. As you release through the doorway, begin to command "Place," leading the dog to the spot you have chosen. When you get to this spot, point

The end result should be a dog whose attention is riveted on the handler and who appears to be happy to work.

When the dog is taught to go to "Place" in a location that is out of the customer's traffic area, everyone is comfortable.

down as in the Down command. Praise with "Good Place!" The first few times you may say "Stay"; however, this practice should be ended quickly.

Start with the dog in place for ten to fifteen minutes and work up to two hours at a time. Of course, if your dog stays quiet or falls asleep, leave well enough alone. If the dog is playing "jack-in-the-box" with you and jumps up every time you turn your back, you will need to work in short sessions. The rule of thumb is the dog gets one mistake and correction. If there is a second mistake, put the dog in a place where you are out of sight for ten to fifteen minutes before you try again. This teaches that if your dog wants to be with you, he/she must do as you wish.

You will generally have a tougher time teaching the Place command to more active breeds (i.e., German Shepherds and Dobermans) than you will have with the larger, slower types such as Rottweilers and Bullmastiffs. In any case, you must be patient and stay the course. Remember that you are working toward the end result.

At four months, you should always use the leash for the Place command, preferably a nylon leash, as the pup will be less likely to chew on nylon than on leather.

PLACE COMMAND—SIX MONTHS

At six months, you should have practiced eight weeks of conditioning using the leash. After you have practiced your basic five Obedience commands off-leash, you are ready to do Place without the leash. Use a tab so that you can correct if and when it is needed.

Now, when you both go through the door, tell your pup to Place, so the dog is not going there with you. If you need to get part of the way, point to the spot. Your ultimate goal is to get the dog to go to Place automatically and alone. Once there, the dog should remain, until released. You can help the dog enjoy a place by making it comfortable. If it is on the tile, make it warm in the winter by using a blanket, rug or bed. During the summer months, the tile is cool. Give the dog something safe to chew on, and from time to time also give a treat. This way, your dog will find satisfaction without moving from the spot. It is also wise to periodically use verbal praise. Give plenty of physical attention so there is no necessity for the pup to get up to seek attention.

SUGGESTIONS FOR THE DOG'S PLACE

Keep your dog out of the path of travel. The place should not be in your normal line of traffic. In a retail setting, the dog should be behind a counter or out of the way of customers where there is enough room to stretch out. Designate a place where the dog can see you, will not try to move in order to see you and will be out of the way. Ideal places include:

- Behind a counter in a store environment
- Behind a desk in an office environment
- In the owner's area rather than the patrons' area
- In an open crate out of the way

The dog's place should be in the owner's work area rather than where the patrons of the business move about. This is for liability reasons as well as the fact that all of your patrons may not be comfortable around the dog.

If adhered to on a regular basis, office and home manners will help to keep the dog *subordinate but not submissive* within the workplace, and will squelch the tendency for stubborn and willful behavior that can be a problem with the kind of temperament a protection dog must have.

CHAPTER VIII

PRACTICAL EXERCISES AND AGILITY

Getting a dog ready for the role of Business Security K-9 involves a lot of practice with things the dog will be expected to accept on a daily basis—things that we take for granted, such as loud traffic noise, honking, buses, strangers and slippery surfaces.

PREPROTECTION CONDITIONING

After the dog has finished teething you will want to begin working on prey drive. Molding the puppy at this age is fun and easy. Begin working with burlap sacks with the young pup prior to teething, and cease all forms of tug-of-war while the puppy's teeth are falling out. At five to six months of age, *when the puppy is no longer losing teeth,* you may begin using the puppy tug.

PUPPY TUG WORK

Your goal with the puppy tug will be to get the puppy to hold on with the entire mouth. The farther back into the jaws the material

Use a tie-out or a handler on the end of the leash to hold the young dog on place. Teach the dog to bite deep in the back part of the jaw.

After the dog is biting well, you may slowly turn the head from side to side. This will aid in teaching the dog to turn the head while biting the leg area.

goes, the better the bite will be. The pup should pull and refuse to let go. Always let the puppy win. The tug can be dragged along the ground on the end of a leash, while the puppy gives chase. When the puppy catches and bites the tug, give a little resistance as if the tug were a wounded animal. When the pup gets a strong hold, let go and let the pup run away with the tug as a reward.

When the puppy is very efficient with the chase, catch and run game described above, you will be ready to add a decoy (assistant). Hold the pup on a leash and flat collar while the decoy drags the pup tug. Encourage the pup to catch the tug. After the tug has been caught, the decoy can grab the end and play a short game of tug with the puppy. When the decoy drops the tug, the pup wins.

After the puppy is accustomed to tugging with the decoy, the puppy's head can be slowly turned from side to side. This move helps to teach the puppy to turn its head when biting.

THE NEXT STEP

The next step will involve the puppy being introduced to protection equipment such as the sleeve or the full-body police suit. Most business security K-9s are trained with the police suit. The following steps should be followed with the aid of a professional trainer. There are many ways to ruin a security dog, both by making the dog too aggressive and by devastating the dog and ruining the protection capabilities. A professional trainer's assistance can prevent this from happening. Also, protection equipment is expensive; the police suit alone costs approximately $1,200, so this is not an item a novice is likely to purchase.

If the dog is not mature enough to have a good, strong bite on the tug, do not even attempt work on a sleeve or pants. Some breeds mature into their drives early while others are slower to blossom. Your trainer will let you know when the time is right to advance to a puppy sleeve or pants. Remember to make sure that these sessions are short and fun for the dog.

Step 1

EQUIPMENT:

- Tie-out line (rubber stretch line with brass buckles)
- Protection collar (2 inches wide)
- Harness (optional)

Drag the prey object (i.e., tug, sleeve or pants) in front of the dog with a leash. Drag it in a straight line—just out of reach—so that your dog can chase it. Encourage and cheer the dog on. When your dog does catch the prey, be lavish with praise and let the dog run with it. Keep your leash around your shoulders so that when it is appropriate, you can let the dog carry the prey away. Do this by snapping the leash on and taking the dog off the tie-out.

Once you are successful with this step, you will want to advance to Step 2. Proceed slowly through each of these steps. Some dogs can advance through each step in days, while others take weeks, even months. We encourage you to be patient.

Step 2

The next step is to put on the sleeve or the pants. It is easy to release the sleeve to the dog. The legs are not as easy. Choose to use a jambier (leg sleeve) or start out with only one leg in the pants. As long as the decoy's (assistant's) shoe can slip out of the leg, the person can take the bite. When ready, the decoy can lean out away from the dog and slip off the pants.

In either case, you must get the dog's attention to the desired point of impact. This is accomplished by moving the object back and forth quickly in front of the dog's line of vision, just barely out of reach. You want the dog to jump out toward the arm or leg to try and bite it.

Periodically, the sleeve or leg should swing close enough for the dog to believe that it is possible to make contact. Eventually when the dog is at the peak of excitement, the decoy will step in and take the bite. A short fight without undue pressure should follow by the release of the prey object, whether it be a sleeve or the pants. This should be practiced until the fight is longer and the bite is solid. The dog should be biting hard with full mouth. The handler can help the bite by holding the line tight when the dog bites. This will help the dog to bite down hard or lose the grip. A loose line will cause mouthing as well as release and bite tendencies when the dog does not hold on.

Begin to teach the "Out" now without correction. After the handler releases the sleeve or pants and these are now in the dog's mouth, reach down and grab the leather collar and pull the dog up on the hind legs. This will eventually become uncomfortable, and the dog will drop the equipment. As this happens, say "Out." Every time you do this, you are teaching what the work means.

Step 3

It is easier for a dog to bite someone who is running away than someone who is face to face. When biting sufficiently hard on the tie-out line, the dog should be taken off the line and put on the leash connected to the police collar (2 inches wide) with a heavy brass snap. We highly recommend the use of brass snaps because other snaps break more easily.

The decoy will come out with the equipment and agitate the dog to high intensity. When the decoy says "Go," or signals, the handler releases the dog with the bite command "Fass." When the dog gets to the decoy, the handler will make sure that the leash is tight enough so that when the decoy slips the equipment, the dog will go no further. The dog will gain more and more confidence each time. The dog has scared and chased the decoy down and was rewarded with an article. Therefore, the dog wins!

RIDING IN CARS, TRUCKS AND AIRPLANES

There are two ways in which K-9s can ride: (1) in the fiberglass crate; or (2) in the Place command.

CRATES

The primary use of the crate is for safety reasons. In vehicles, they prevent the dog from flying around in a car or truck in case of an accident. In an open truck, they are a must for the dog's safety as well as for the people who may come too close to the vehicle while it is parked in a parking lot or at a gas station.

In a commercial airline, the crate is the only way your dog is allowed to travel unless it is a service dog (police, rescue, Seeing Eye). In a private aircraft, it is up to the pilot how the dog is shipped. If a crate is not used, it is important that the dog is anchored down to a place well away from the pilot. This is for everyone's safety. In case of turbulence, the pilot, passengers and K-9s are all anchored down.

The crate is also used for cleanliness. If you do not want hair and dirt in your vehicle, the crate provides the solution. Cleaning is much easier when 95 percent of the hair and dirt is kept in the crate. Cleaning is easy, taking only ten minutes when necessary.

THE PLACE COMMAND

You may desire to use your dog for vehicle protection as well as at your place of business. In this case, you should designate a seat or area of the vehicle for the dog. You may want to throw down a blanket or sheet if you do not wish to purchase a professional seat cover.

The dog should be told to "Place" and should be shown the correct spot. If it is necessary to loosely tie the dog the first few times, it is all right to do so, especially if you do not have assistance. If you stay consistent with which seat the dog sits on, this will soon become conditioned behavior.

Entering and exiting the vehicle or aircraft should be handled the same way that door crashing is handled. Require that the dog wait to be told "Okay" before entering or exiting the vehicle.

The crate, when used regularly, becomes a bed or a den for your dog at home or on the road.

The dog should learn to accept unexpected greetings from strangers.

PUBLIC TRANSPORTATION

Because they are defensive by nature, K-9s, in general, should not be put into situations where they are cramped into tight quarters with strangers. With the possible exception of the more mild-mannered store mascot, buses, subways and trains should be avoided whenever possible. In some instances, a dog is not permitted on public transportation unless it is a service dog.

THE DOG IN PUBLIC

The security K-9 who has a job description that entails dealing with the public must be mannerly. The dog will need to get used to being out of the home environment from puppyhood. You must make it a point, at least once a week, to take the puppy or young dog on an outing. Your goal should be to frequent public areas long enough for you to see the puppy or dog become noticeably tired, bored or indifferent to all of the activity. This is to condition the dog not to become overly nervous or excited in public. Shopping centers, downtown business and shopping areas, particularly during lunch hours or close of business, are good places to take the dog.

STREET NOISE AND ENCOUNTERING STRANGERS

You will want the puppy to become accustomed to the sounds of large trucks and traffic honking. It is important that the puppy learn about elevators, escalators (be careful of the paws), automatic doors and so on. Practice Sit and Down/Stays near an automatic door. **Do not take the dog off-leash or leave the dog.** Make the dog stop at all curbs and wait to be told "Okay" before stepping into the street. This is a safety precaution and helps to reinforce the danger of the street to the dog.

The business security K-9 should be well socialized in the first year of life so that strangers will not trigger a fear-aggression response. The dog will, however, be conditioned not to automatically trust a stranger so it will be important not to allow people to over-whelm the dog.

As previously stated, it is not wise to allow your patrons to pet the dog. The dog's training will be undermined unless the dog's job is "mascot," in which case undermining the training is not a serious factor.

The dog should be conditioned to stay separate and quiet when around strangers. Being watchful is an asset and should never be discouraged, but being distracted should be discouraged. If your dog is going through a difficult period in its development where control problems develop for the handler, *the dog should be left at home until the problems are worked out.* The dog may be brought along, but crated for safety and control. **Caution:** Remember, dogs do not possess the ability to reason; they react largely on instinct and conditioned responses. Two things that can confuse a dog and elicit the wrong response follow:

1. People wearing ski clothing (i.e., parkas, ski suits, etc.) because they resemble bite suits. In general this is not a problem, but it is advisable to be aware.
2. People swinging sticks, bats, crutches or any object that could be construed as a weapon in the direction of a family member.

Avoiding these problems is part of awareness, which is most important to the K-9 owner/handler.

DISTRACTION WORK AND POISON PROOFING

Overcoming distractions is an important part of the security K-9's training. This is important because if the dog cannot learn to focus on the job at hand and ignore outside influences, the dog may let you down under real stress or distractions. A distraction can be just about anything that is likely to get your dog's attention. Distractions that are the most typical are what you want to proof

On an Out command the dog should sit by the handler's side and remain calm.

On one word from the handler the same dog should believe that the intentions of this man are hostile and the dog should react appropriately.

the most. Of particular interest to dogs are new smells, quick movement (animals or people) and unique or frightening noises, however any or all of the following could be considered distractions to your dog: a rolling ball, another dog or animal, cooking food, food offered, loud noises, traffic sounds, gunfire, metal objects, wood falling and especially the things that are in your particular environment. For instance, if you own a car repair business, you will want to proof your dog around cars.

Poison proofing is a must for most business security K-9s. The dog needs to receive a negative association with taking food from a stranger or off the ground.

A certain amount of poison proofing can be accomplished by using food in association with agitation and refusal during Obedience training. The use of a fence charger (livestock), which is connected to the foil holding food, is the surest way to poison-proof. Food is left out randomly at various distances. The wire should be long so that it can stretch out a distance of 50 to 100 feet, and coated so that the dog will not receive a shock. Only the food area has a current associated with it. The dog should make an association between a stranger offering food and shock. This will prevent the dog from being won over by food.

CLIMBING, JUMPING AND BALANCING

Agility helps to build the dog's confidence. The dog should learn how to climb, jump, balance, crawl and so on. The standard catwalk, jumps and tunnels can be utilized, but you can also use things that are available to you as long as they are safe. The idea is to build confidence and teach the dog how to go over, through, under and around things quickly, should the dog ever need to.

You can use wooden playground equipment, chairs, hedges, small fences and large pipes. Go slowly and build on small successes. Be happy if the dog tries one or two new things at a time. Have the dog jump 2 feet before you try 3, 4 or more. Slow and steady finishes the "race," an injured dog doesn't.

CHAPTER IX

LEVEL 1—ALARM, DETERRENT AND THREAT TRAINING

Whether you desire to utilize your K-9 as an alarm/deterrent or for threat and defense purposes, you will need to begin the security K-9's training with civil defense work. The result you attain after this training will be determined (all things being equal) by the dog's protection temperament and defense drive. The dog with a 7–7½ protection temperament will learn how to alarm to danger and, by alarming, act as a deterrent. The 8–9½ temperament will back the same situation up with defense.

The dog sport enthusiast who reads this will need to do so with an open mind. While we teach some of the same techniques, we do so from a different perspective and for a different purpose.

Until this chapter, we have focused on how to prepare the dog for protection training. It is now time to begin to teach the art of K-9 protection.

Defense is very important to the business protection or security patrol K-9. This dog should have a naturally suspicious nature. The primary difference in Schutzhund sport is the importance of the equipment. In dog sport, the equipment is the dog's focal point. If given the chance, the sport dog will attack the equipment if it is left on the ground. The dog is worked primarily out of the Prey Drive and this desire to bite an object reflects this point. There are, of course, dogs that compete in European sports that are also naturally high in Defense; but, in general, it is not a necessity to do well in competition.

On the other hand, the business protection or security patrol dog is at a loss without a good deal of Defense Drive. The best *sport* dogs are typically 60 percent Prey driven and 40 percent Defense driven. Conversely, the best business protection candidates work at about 60 percent Defense and 40 percent Prey Drive. If the percentage of the Prey Drive goes any higher or the Defense Drive any lower, you will have a dog that perhaps looks good on the field, but in real situations will not be naturally defensive enough. In the case of a dog going lower in Prey Drive and higher in Defense, you may have a very good patrol dog, but one you can never fully trust with people. Therefore, sticking to a 60:40 ratio is your best bet.

COMMANDS

The dog can learn any language you wish, as long as it is consistent. Since most people in the United States use either English or German commands (because of German importing throughout the years), we will limit ourselves to the following examples:

OBEDIENCE COMMANDS

ENGLISH	GERMAN
Heel	Fuss
Sit	Sitz
Come	Hier
Down	Platz
No	Pfui
Good dog	Das in fine

PROTECTION COMMANDS

ENGLISH	GERMAN
Watch 'em	Pass-auf
Speak	Gib laut
Hunt, Check	Revier
Bite	Packen
Hold	Fass
Out	Aus

EQUIPMENT NEEDED

1. 2-inch-wide leather police collar
2. German steel choke
3. 6-foot-long (1-inch-wide) police leash with brass clip preferred. Leash can be leather or double-layer nylon.
4. 30-foot-long line (half-inch wide) with brass clip preferred
5. Leather or nylon loop-style tab; 6–10 inches in length
6. Tie-out line with rubber connector in center to allow for give
7. Agitation stick or whip—preferably a noisemaker (clatter stick or whip)

Do not allow the dog to eat or drink large amounts of water before or soon after training. It is better to train a dog with an empty stomach as there is a danger of the stomach twisting (gastric torsion), which can be fatal.

WHAT IS THREAT TRAINING?

Threat training is the process of teaching the dog to act out aggressively to protect a business, home, yard, car and owner. During threat training, we work primarily with the dog's Defensive Drive. The dog's Prey Drive is only used in the sense that as the intruder retreats, the dog gains confidence and wants to give chase.

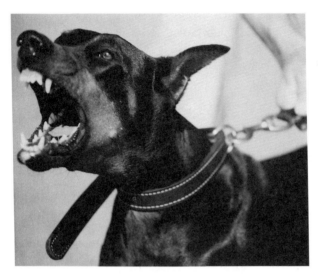

Although she appears willing to bite, "Kim" is a 7¹/₂ on the temperament scale. She is simply displaying the Defense she has been taught through level 1 protection training. This is pure defense; this dog is not a candidate for bite work.

The Giant Schnauzer displays the face of a dog in threat training. Note the two collars: a training collar high on the neck for control and the police collar low on the neck to protect the neck from stress due to pulling.

It is just as important (if not more so) that during this stage of training, we also teach the dog to *cease aggression on command.* This is *unconditional control* on command. The dog must learn that **the owner is ultimately in control of any aggression.**

There are a number of reasons why we teach threat training before bite training:

1. The dog is leaning to be truly aggressive toward the intruder. The dog is not taking cues because of the presence of equipment.
2. Since the dog has had many rewarding hours by now, playfully biting and tugging on the puppy tug, we want to change the attitude from play to true defensiveness. The presence of the puppy tug at this point will only serve to bring back the idea of play.
3. Once the dog's defensiveness is well established, we can begin to teach the "Out," which means to cease aggression. When the owner calls "Out," the dog should stop barking, growling and lunging. At this point, the dog should sit and behave unless attacked or told otherwise. We have found that teaching the Out in this manner cuts your work in half later on when you teach the dog to Out from the bite.

CAN YOU TEACH THE DOG ONLY LEVEL I PROTECTION AND OPT NOT TO PROGRESS ANY FURTHER?

YES! Many feel that this is enough training for their needs and will opt not to proceed with bite work. This is acceptable if all that is desired is a cosmetic look of aggression behind a fence or other barrier. If your threat assessment is not high or your dog is not a "hard dog" (one possessing strong nerves and temperament), this may be all you want or can expect from the dog.

However, we must caution that you should not choose this option out of fear of teaching the dog how to bite. If your dog has a solid temperament, teaching how to apprehend someone will not create a dangerous animal. Quite the contrary. If handled properly, bite training will give the dog confidence and teach control. This can be compared to martial arts classes. They do not create bullies, but rather people who have a quiet confidence and the ability to act if necessary.

Again, it is important to emphasize that *we must have a well-rounded, stable-minded trio of dog, owner and trainer* to achieve the desired end result.

WON'T A WELL-BRED DOG BE NATURALLY DEFENSIVE ENOUGH?

This is a misconception held by many people. In reality, most people over- or underestimate their dog's propensity for aggression. This can lead to accidents or disappointments. A dog left alone to figure out what to do is likely to do the wrong thing. Police officers have reported that many rapes, burglaries and beatings have taken place with the family dog nearby. The reason for inappropriate action are numerous, not the least of which is lack of training.

When startled, a dog is faced with two options: fight or flight. If untrained, a dog will make the choice in a split second. Quite frankly, you are just plain lucky if the dog chooses to come to your aid without being taught how to respond.

Liability is the other hazard in this way of thinking. *The vast majority of accidental dog bites are from untrained dogs.* The dogs often are encouraged by their owners to be aggressive until they become neighborhood bullies. The dogs are now fully defensive, but are they controllable? *Dogs demonstrating uncontrolled aggression are a definite liability.* We have trained dogs for clients who were at the point where no one would come to visit because of the fear of their dogs. The rule of thumb here is, if you rely on your dog as a form of protection, train for it! You will have increased by 70 to 90 percent the chance of your dog acting appropriately when needed.

ARE THERE DOGS THAT WILL TURN ON THEIR OWNERS?

There are three factors that can make a dog turn on the owner:

1. POOR OR ABUSIVE TRAINING OR HANDLING
2. Poor breeding—dog with low stress level
3. Medical/clinical problem (i.e., brain tumor, etc.)

During training, a dog can be overstressed to the point of becoming uncontrollably defensive. We call this dog a fear-biter—one who has learned that defense is the answer to all fears. This dog has a hair trigger—a common result of novice training and/or bad breeding. Breeding dogs with poor temperaments can result in dogs with natural fear-biting tendencies. A dog with a low stress level who is taken into protection training will "stress out" and attempt to bite anything available (including the owner). We recommend that this dog never enter a protection program.

■ ■ ■

Personally, when we encounter a dog we feel is dangerous, we write a statement of our findings and have the owner sign it. We recommend that such a dog be kept in a secure dog run unless under the owner's immediate supervision or on a leash. In extreme cases, we have had to recommend that certain dogs be put to sleep because of their viciousness. This happens most often when an owner of a two-to-four-year-old dog with no training brings the animal to us and says, "Can you fix him?"

■ ■ ■

If you follow the program we have laid out for you in this book, this is a problem you will not encounter.

SAFETY COLLAR

The safety collar is an extra collar attached to the tie-out just in case the first collar breaks. Judging the aggressiveness and strength of the dog, you may even utilize a second safety line.

THREAT TRAINING

FOCUS ON THE INTRUDER/ATTACKER

Step 1 Goal: Teaching the Dog to be Alert and Bark on Command

Wearing a 2-inch leather collar, the dog should be anchored to the tie-out line. The safety collar (large choke collar) should also be loosely attached. The dog is held by the handler at the end of the line in the Heel position. The dog does not have to sit or perform any Obedience tasks.

On "Go," the agitator approaches in a manner consistent with the temperament of the dog (i.e., at a distance for a weak civil dog, closer for a strong civil dog). The decoy moves in a quick, jerky motion to attract the dog's attention. To the dog, the decoy seems to appear aggressive and fearful at the same time. A skilled decoy knows how to seemingly challenge one moment and to jump back fearfully the next, all with body language.

With the first sign of aggression or forward movement (on the part of the dog), the decoy pulls in and runs for the hills. The handler verbally lavishes praise on the dog when the decoy is present and then physically when the decoy is out of sight. This builds the dog's confidence and quickly teaches the dog to relieve the stress of the situation with forward motion, a bark or a growl. Timing is critical when teaching the dog the meaning of the commands. When the decoy first appears, you should tell your dog to be alert by saying "On Guard" or "Pass-auf" (German). Your dog will begin to look for trouble in association with your warning.

Some breeds are much more inclined than others when it comes to barking. German Shepherd Dogs, for instance, are much more likely to bark quickly than Rottweilers. The command for bark is "Gib laut" (German). We say "Watch 'em" (English). These are typical commands; however, you can use anything you like, *but be consistent.*

The tie-out line is a special nylon line with a rubber strap in the middle to absorb the shock of the dog's pulling. This line also prevents handler error that can result in injury to the decoy.

One Training Session

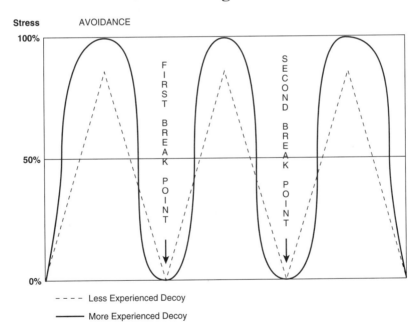

This diagram shows a typical protection training session involving three encounters. The solid line shows how the experienced decoy can work the dog right up to its peak without putting the dog into avoidance. The perforated line is the less experienced decoy who should not attempt to push the dog as hard or as fast because a mistake could result in a loss of confidence on the dog's part.

Step 2 Goal: Teaching the Dog to Cease Aggression on Command

Once the dog will alert on command and bark on command, we will need to teach "Out" (English) or "Aus" (German). This means to cease aggression and behave. We command the dog "Out" and "Sit."

This step may need to be initiated as early as the third day of threat training for a hard (aggressive) dog, and possibly as late as three weeks for a soft (less aggressive) dog. This time the dog also wears a training collar, a steel choke—typically the same type used for Obedience. This is worn around the throat above the police collar. The 6-foot line is attached to the training collar. The line is not held tight, as you must be careful *not to correct* when the dog is on the alert or bark command.

On cue, the decoy will cease agitation. You should command the dog "Out." From this point on, when aggressive, the dog is corrected with "No" and a jerk, which should be remembered from Obedience.

Next, give the command "Sit" and praise. At this point, pet the dog on the head or scratch behind the ear. As the dog is soothed and remains calm, repeat "Out, good Out." The decoy should be able to casually walk by, back and forth, as the handler keeps the dog under control.

Step 3 Goal: Teaching the Dog to Trust Your Judgment

Now that the dog understands the concept commands of Alert, Bark and Out, it is important to teach the trust of your judgment and your commands. The dog now understands being aggressive toward *other* aggressive behavior and being calm on "Out" when things calm down. The question becomes: what if there is a need to be aggressive when things calm, or clam when things seem aggressive? The only way for you to ensure this behavior is to proceed to the next two steps: "friendly agitation" and "agitating Outs."

Friendly Agitation

Friendly agitation involves teaching the dog to trust your judgment and not to trust anyone else. Throughout their lives, most dogs have learned that a person acting friendly is a friendly person. This can work against you if your assailant decides not to speak loudly or to move quickly. It is possible to be threatened with a weapon or verbally assaulted without the gestures that might cue your dog. It is not unusual for the potential stalker to assess your dog and try to sweet-talk or get past the animal with a tidbit. This is why it is so important to teach the dog that your judgment is all that matters. *Remember, dogs do not have the ability to reason. Therefore, legally it is important that the dog listen to you unconditionally.*

Using both police and training collars, the dog (again on the tree) is approached by the decoy. The first agitation will be typical aggressive agitation followed by an "Out" for control.

Next, the decoy will approach in a friendly manner by sweet-talking and patting his or her knee with hand extended as if to offer the dog a treat. During this time, the handler gives the dog *aggressive cues* ("Pass-auf" and "Gib laut"). Typically, the dog will fall for it at least one time. The dog will be confused but will most likely give in to the stronger conditioning, which is to trust. The handler then tells the dog "No," "Pass-auf," "Gib laut." At this point, the decoy will show true intentions and tap the dog on the nose or ear and then jump back. The dog will quickly realize the handler was right and that he (the dog) has been suckered.

Repeat this process until the dog no longer buys into the sucker routine. Do not be surprised at first if the dog tends to be more aggressive on friendly agitation, as this is a typical reaction to a loss of innocence.

Step 4 Goal: Teaching the Dog Agitating Outs

Now that we have taught the dog to listen to your judgment in what seems to be a friendly situation, we will throw the dog another curve by teaching that all seemingly aggressive acts are not necessarily what they appear to be. The decoy will approach the dog, who is once again on the line and wearing both collars. The dog is commanded to "Out" and is soothed. The decoy jogs by at a rapid pace, sparking the dog's Prey Drive. The decoy then may turn quickly and with raised arms. Your decoy has the option to approach the dog and scamper away, reach to pet the dog and quickly pull back or yell, scream and hit a bush with the stick—just about anything except for directing aggression toward the dog.

During this time, the handler of the dog should be controlling the dog with command "Out" and praise "Good dog" and "Good Out" and the strong controlled correction "No" anytime the dog presumes to make an independent judgment.

Step 5 Goal: Holding the Dog Back— The Handler in Control

Once all of the steps are followed and the dog is listening properly to all cues, you are ready to remove the tie-out line.

Now the *handler* is responsible for holding the dog back rather than a tree and tie-out line. Before giving the handler this responsibility, it is best to talk the handler through proper stance. The training director should give the person the leash and request that it be held as if the dog were attached. Grab the leash and give it a yank equal to what the dog might give. The handler should remain planted. Handlers should be taught to center themselves if they move forward and to absorb the shock without moving.

The dog should now wear the police collar held by the police leash. The training collar should have a 10-inch tab connected to it and the leash should be run through the loop of the tab to the protection collar. The other option is the police circular leash with a clasp on each end. As the handler assumes control of the dog physically, you will run systematically through all of the steps.

■ ■ ■

Note: All agitation sessions should be *short,* as your dog expends a great deal of energy during this process. There is a lot of mental

Jerre Freeman readies her dog for the bite.

Using the full-body bite suit, decoy and handler can teach the dog to apprehend any part of the body.

stress on the dog as well. It is not unusual to work a dog on each series only three to six times. You can negate your training by over-working or overstressing the dog.

■ ■ ■

Some critics may think it unnecessary to teach the dog not to trust. The reality is that these dogs are expected to face real-life situations. The majority of human beings learn sometime in adult lives not to trust strangers. It is only natural to teach a protection dog not to trust strangers no matter what the ploy.

BUILDING SEARCH

Purpose: To teach the dog to check the place of business for intruders and to warn the owner of people hiding there.

Prior to teaching this command, we should have worked on all of the other avenues of civil defense around the business.

Now go to the front of the business area and hold the dog (facing the business) with the usual equipment (police and training collars) setup. The decoy approaches from the front of the business and agitates the dog. When the dog is sufficiently worked up, the decoy runs into the business and hides in a predesignated place. After giving the decoy sufficient time to hide, the handler takes the dog into the business and gives the command "Check." In the beginning, we will intersperse this command with "Watch 'em, Check," since the Check command is new and we want the dog to remain on track.

When you enter the business, how quickly the dog finds the intruder will indicate how natural it is for the dog to use the sense of scent. Other people should not be in the business confines, as a serious accident could result if someone startles the dog. The animal should be intent on looking for the intruder. The first find should be fairly easy and set up. Upon entering the business, you should be cognizant of two factors: air circulation and quartering the area.

Air Circulation

It will much more difficult for the dog to find an intruder if the air conditioning is on, because the scent will then be circulating in various directions. Turn off all fans and remove any unnecessary distracting scents from the area, as this is very distracting to the dog.

Quartering the Area

Even though this is a training setup, we must teach the handler proper procedures in case of a real-life situation. When entering a business, each room has to be cleared *systematically* before moving on. This is important so the intruder does not end up behind you. Pay close attention to the dog's cues. After you have practiced with this dog many times, you will begin to understand the dog's indications. Typically, a dog will become excited and begin to pull into the leash, with tail up and head down, in order to scent. Do not pull your dog away from the scent. Trust the dog!

In most cases, if you believe someone is in your business, you should leave and call the police. It is extremely dangerous for both you and your dog to go in. You must remember that *a protection dog is meant to be used defensively, not offensively!* Even a police unit uses caution when sending a K-9 in after a hidden suspect, because there is no way of knowing if this person is armed.

It is wise to announce at the door that the intruder should come out or the K-9 will be sent in. Do not do this unless you are armed and prepared should the intruder come out shooting. Your best bet is to back off and call the police. If the dog is allowed to check the business and does locate the intruder, the dog should give a strong indication that the person is hidden behind the door or wherever.

During this portion of training, the handler pulls the dog back and the decoy comes out agitating the dog. When the dog's aggression peaks, the decoy turns and runs. The handler and the dog give chase, stopping at the doorway.

You must be very careful to give the decoy a good head start. While training is taking place inside, doors should remain open for easy escape. This is very scary for the decoy. Even if 20 feet behind, it feels as if the dog is right on top of the decoy.

GETTING PAST THE DOG

Our real-life experience with the bad elements of society points out certain procedures they typically employ. Most stalkers assess their target's vulnerability prior to attacking. This is why you want a potential stalker to see that the dog is with you. This alone will force a stalker to think twice about choosing you as a target. Try not to be predictable as to when you leave the dog outside or in your home. The more time and effort necessary to get at you, the less likely a stalker is to bother you.

CASE HISTORY

We had a client who initially called us after being raped in her own home. She was a widow who lived alone in a beautiful home in a nice neighborhood in Orange County, California. She said she had not been too concerned about her safety in general because she lived in a nice area—a common misconception. She had purchased a German Shepherd Dog because of the "night stalker" who had been on the loose the previous year in Southern California. Following the night stalker's subsequent capture, her fears subsided and she chose not to follow through with the dog's training. What she did not know was that she was being watched and another stalker knew that her dog was left outside at night.

One night, the woman was awakened by the dog's frantic barking. She guessed (incorrectly) that the dog was responding to a cat on the fence and promptly fell back asleep. In actuality, the dog was responding to someone who had opened the garage door and was attempting to gain access into her home. She was startled awake by a man's hand covering her mouth. She fought him and managed to bolt downstairs. Her single thought was to let the dog in the house. The dog was now lunging at the back door. Although untrained, the dog was desperately trying to help the owner. Unfortunately, she was caught by the man, and raped, beaten and robbed only 15 feet from her dog. She was fortunate to survive this ordeal.

Since then the dog has been trained for protection and now sleeps next to her at night. If the dog had been previously left inside, the stalker most likely would have gone elsewhere. In any case, the stalker would have had to go through the dog to get to her. At the very least, she would have had a chance.

LEARNING CURVES

It is important to understand that in protection training, the dog will go through peaks and valleys. It is not unusual for a dog to be excellent one day and terrible the next. This is why the decoy's and training director's roles are so vital. They must decide when to go forward and when to back off. For both physical and psychological reasons, dogs are ever-changing creatures and must be evaluated from day to day. The best trainers will instinctively know how far they can take dogs before pushing them into avoidance. A dog will need to be monitored carefully for a minimum of two years until settled into training. The period of time between one and two years of age is the most erratic for a young dog, who is just becoming an individual and figuring out what to do with natural drives. This is why it is so important to stabilize aggression early.

BUSINESS SITUATION SETUPS

Situation setups are the most important aspect of a successful K-9 training program. This is the only way for you to know if your K-9 is reliable. This process will give you insight into the strengths and weaknesses of your K-9. Each situation you can foresee should be practiced If you know what type of threat you are most likely to encounter, these are the scenarios you should practice. Examples are:

1. Assault on the way to the business place
2. Assault while opening the store
3. Verbal or physical assault in the business place
4. Assault while closing the store
5. Assault on the street
6. Carjacking—assault in the car
7. Property theft

Each situation should be set up as realistically as possible.

CHAPTER X

LEVELS 2 AND 3— APPREHENSION WORK ON AND OFF LEASH

LEVEL 2 APPREHENSION WORK (ON-LEASH 6 TO 30 FEET)

Up to this point, we have not used equipment in our agitation. This is because we want to fix the dog's mind firmly on the decoy intruder or agitator. Equipment would distract from this process. Now, because of necessity, we must return to the use of the following equipment:

1. Full-body police bite suit of European design
2. German sleeves—puppy, intermediate and advanced
3. Agitation sticks—bamboo, whip and reed
4. Tie-out line
5. Collars—training collars, 2-inch police collar
6. Leashes—6-foot leash, 30-foot-long line

Although German sleeves can be used, it is recommended that you use a full-body police bite suit for realism and versatility. You should only conduct bite training with the assistance of a professional trainer. The trainer should have all of the pieces of equipment you will need for training.

The police suit is designed to be as formfitting as possible while allowing the most protection possible for decoy. When proper technique is applied by the decoy, the material will slip away from the skin as the dog bites

On-Leash Apprehension Work

Step 1: Teaching the Bite—Slipping Equipment

By this time, you should have had plenty of experience teaching the dog the skills of biting and head turning with the puppy tug. If you have somehow missed this step, you will need to cover it here before you move on.

The next move will be to introduce the biting *equipment,* which will be the pants, the jacket or the sleeve, depending upon the dog and your purpose. In any case, your goal is to teach the dog to bite the equipment and bite it powerfully. In order to do this, we must switch the focus of attention from the Defensive Drive to the Prey Drive. To accomplish this, we will temporarily separate the equipment from the person.

Take the biting equipment and swing it in front of the dog in a teasing fashion. The dog is finally rewarded with the equipment after a short tug-of-war, and should then be allowed to carry the equipment away. This can (and should) be done with *both* the *tie-out line* and the handler holding the *leash.* There are advantages and disadvantages to both. The tie-out makes it easier for the decoy to work safely and to create a better bite by the dog straining on the line. The handler holding the leash helps to improve confidence by allowing the dog to carry the prey (equipment) away.

Step 2: Teaching Out and Guard

Put the equipment on *only* after you feel the dog is committed to the equipment. You do not want the dog to concentrate on your face or hands as in a defensive mode. You want your dog looking straight at the target area on the equipment.

To do this, the decoy must ensure that the target is moving and is the most obvious thing about the decoy. The target must move horizontally across the dog's plane of vision. *If it is the arm,* we swing it in a sideways motion across the body and in front of the dog's field of view. *If it is a leg,* we must kick out to the side, offering the leg just below the knee to the dog. This looks like a martial arts side kick or a soccer kick.

It is very important that the handler hold the dog down on all fours when teaching leg bites. Locking your elbow with your hand close to the collar will prevent the dog from being able to go up high on the decoy. To concentrate on the legs, the decoy cannot wear the jacket; therefore, this technique is very important for safety. Once the dog has a good hold, the decoy must keep the prey (equipment) moving in order to keep the dog focused. When the decoy stops fighting, the handler grabs the dog's collar and holds the dog up off the front paws. The dog lets go when the handler commands "Out," causing the dog to release the bite.

At this point, the handler sits the dog right in front of the decoy. While holding the dog in position, the handler should tell the dog to guard the decoy. When the decoy attempts to get away, the handler gives the command to bite again and the dog is given the equipment as a reward. If the decoy cannot slip out of the pants, you must give the "Out" command to the dog and have the decoy jump out of reach.

Step 3: Bite, Out, Guard and Reattack

In this step, the dog comes off the tie-out and is held by the handler. The dog who has learned on the legs until now must be taught an extra step—that is, to bite the jacket as well. When the dog comes off the tie-out, it is important for the decoy's safety to wear the jacket. For the first time, the team will practice the basic series in protection: Bite, Out.

The handler holds the leash tight in order to set the bite.

The dog watches the decoy for any sign of escape while the handler searches for weapons, etc.

Guard and Reattack

Holding the dog, the handler waits for the decoy to agitate the dog and come for the bite. The decoy fights with the dog and then freezes. On cue from the decoy, the handler gives the "Out" command and tells the dog to "Sit" and "Guard." If there is difficulty with the Out, the handler corrects the dog forward *into the bite, not away from it.* This is to protect the dog's teeth from harm.

The handler sits the dog in front of the decoy with the "Guard" command. When the decoy makes a move, the dog will reattack. At first you can help with a German bite word—"Packen" or "Fass." However, later you will not have to. The dog must be cheered and praised for every correct action.

Following the reattack, the dog may be given the equipment. However, this time, after the dog's brief enjoyment of the reward, the decoy will return threatening the dog. The handler will bring the dog back *on the decoy rather than the equipment.* The timing of this move is very important and should not be done at all if the dog is biting softly.

Step 4: 6-Foot Leash—Basic Series and Transport

The dog is now familiar with the entire series of moves. We must teach dogs not to anticipate only one attempted escape. We will begin to have the dog defend against one to three escapes at random. This way, a dog knows never to stop watching the decoy until the handler gives a command to come away or go to the Heel position.

The escapes can happen at any time. They can occur just after the dog releases the bite, during the handler's search of the decoy for weapons or during the transport. Once the dog learns this, it will not be assumed that the decoy is passive after being stopped by the dog.

To practice this, the handler will send the dog on the bite to the end of a 6-foot line and will then command the dog "Out" and guard. Here the decoy has the option to attempt to escape. The handler will then proceed to leave the dog's side after the decoy's hands are raised. At this point, many handlers prefer to put the dog on a Down and guard. It helps to ensure holding the position and gives the decoy valuable seconds to bring his or her arms down if the dog springs. This is a time when the decoy's stomach can be vulnerable if the dog goes under the jacket.

The handler steps behind the decoy and takes the agitation stick. At this time, the decoy may attempt an escape. The handler then returns to the dog, gives the command "Heel" and takes the dog to the decoy's right Heel position. Now the dog is between the handler and decoy. The handler now commands the decoy to walk forward. As they walk together in a line, the dog should be aware that *the decoy can make a break for it*. If this happens *the dog must reattack*. The decoy is transported to the training director and the exercise is complete.

Step 5: 30-Foot-Long Line Series and Transport

The next step is practicing the same series with random escapes, but with the dog working at a distance of up to 30 feet. This is the step that will separate the mediocre dogs from the truly courageous animals. The only thing that is different here from all previous work is that you are no longer fighting side by side with your dog. Now you are sending the dog to fight alone with only your verbal encouragement from behind.

For some dogs, this makes no difference whatsoever. With others, this is a devastating turn of events. If your dog has difficulty with distance, work slowly and gradually increase the distance. You can still work off-leash, but what you are seeing is a lack of self-confidence. This generally will not happen if the dog is genetically well bred for working, has a good relationship with the owner and has had sound training.

The dog should keep her eyes on the decoy at all times during the side transport.

BUILDING SEARCH—THE BARK AND HOLD

Now that we have taught the dog how to bite, we must teach a second command to just hold someone. We use the English word "Check." You may also use "Search," "Hunt," or "Find," "Revier" (German). This word should mean locate, bark and hold to the dog unless the person moves.

STEP 1: DECOY COMES TO DOG

As with any other command, we must first show the dog what we want. In order to do this, the decoy approaches the dog slowly and methodically. The dog should be encouraged to bark and carry on, but at the same time the handler should hold the dog short and praise. The decoy eventually should be within reach of the dog, but as the decoy is not moving, the dog maintains a Speak and Hold. After the dog gives several intense bark, the dog is rewarded with the Bite.

STEP 2: HANDLER AND DOG GO TO DECOY WITH 6-FOOT LEASH

After the dog knows the Check command (meaning only to bark until the decoy moves), you are ready to take the dog to the decoy. You execute basically the same thing in reverse as in Step 1. This time you give the command and you proceed slowly (although the dog will be quicker than the decoy in Step 1) to the decoy and encourage the dog to bark and hold. Again, when the decoy moves, the dog is rewarded with the Bite.

STEP 3: BARK AND HOLD ON 30-FOOT LINE

Now that the dog has the idea firmly ingrained that "Check" means to go to the decoy and bark and hold, you are ready to let the dog go faster *and without you* close behind.

Starting 15 feet away from the decoy, send the dog on a Check command. Just as the dog gets to the decoy, tighten the leash so that a bite is not possible. Encourage and calm your dog at the

Using the long line the dog gets used to biting at a distance from the handler.

The dog also gets used to guarding the suspect at a distance from the handler.

If the dog is handler-sensitive and attempts to return to the handler rather than guard the suspect, two long lines can be used to hold the dog in place, as shown here.

same time. You may need to control, pet and soothe the dog. You may have to tell the dog "Gib laut" or whatever bark command you use. The dog must bark six to twelve times before getting rewarded by being able to bite.

LEVEL 3 APPREHENSION WORK (OFF-LEASH)

BODY BITES AND FALL DOWNS

Now that the dog has learned the basics of personal protection, we can intensify training. Your dog has been in serious protection training for four to six months by now and should be reasonably self-confident. We are now ready to teach a more advanced style that will involve teaching body bites, transfers, stick hits, kicks, obstacle and noise distractions.

Step 1: On-Leash Body Bites and Fall Downs

This phase of training teaches the dog to be versatile about where the bite is given. It is now up to the decoy to present different body biting areas for the dog. The shoulder can be given by a simple half turn at the correct time. The exposed body part is the shoulder. Since the shoulder is up high, once the dog bites, he or she should be picked up and then set down to recover strength, after which the dog can be picked up again. Practice should also take place on the inside of the arms, the stomach, the back, the backs of the legs and the rear end of the decoy.

Now to add some realism to the sounds of protection work. The decoy should begin to scream and yell. The dog can be taught that if hit properly, the decoy will fall to the ground. This is an excellent confidence builder for the dog. It is essential that when the decoy goes down, the handler be there to protect the decoy's face. This is accomplished by putting the handler between the dog and the decoy's face before calling the dog off. One should *never* call the dog off a decoy on the ground before the handler has control of the dog. The chance of the dog going into the decoy's face is very high if the handler is not right there to control the situation.

Step 2: Long-Line Preparations for Off-Leash Bites

As previously stated, the long-line work will display the true working qualities of the dog. A truly hard dog will not have any problems with the presence of the long line. On the other hand, the soft dog may balk at it and may hesitate to drag the line or leave your side. You will have to eliminate the line for this dog and work on the light line or off-leash at this point. It will not matter much because this dog is generally very obedient and controlled on the Outs. Building this dog's intensity and confidence is the problem. Therefore, you will need to do a lot of runaway work with this kind of dog.

A more common problem is that the dog does not "feel" the Out (letting go) until the handler is right there. There are generally three ways of correcting the dog's way of thinking:

- Handler correction, with long line
- Training director correction, with long line
- Decoy correction, with leash

Step 3: Light-Line Work with Stick Hits and Distractions

The dog is now ready to progress to the light line or Toy breed leash. By this time, the dog should be solid on all commands. However, the line is here just in case we need to apply a correction.

The decoy begins by putting more pressure on the dog in the form of stick hits and kicks. *A good decoy knows how to do this without hurting the dog.* The dog is NEVER hit on the head, and is only struck on the sides or the thick muscles of the back. Because the sticks are made of lightweight reed and bamboo materials, and because of the dog's thick coat, *the animal is not harmed in any way.* As for kicks, they are only of *minimum strength* with the side of the foot. Our intention is to teach the dog what may be encountered, not to discourage. ***Hurting the dog would defeat the purpose.***

189

THE BUSINESS SECURITY K-9

It is time to be creative. The decoy may choose to block the dog's path with various articles, bang trash cans, topple chairs, throw wads of paper at the dog, throw a cup of water or play matador and miss when the dog comes in for a bite. A certain amount of this is good for the dog. It is up to the experienced decoy and training director to know when the dog has had enough.

Step 4: Off-Leash Situations

Now is the time to take off the leash and only have the tab on the collar just in case you need the control. If the dog still shows an occasional lack of willingness to Out, the handler may want to knot a choke chain and use it as a throw chain toward the dog's hindquarters. Sometimes it works to have a third party do this so the dog can never be sure where the correction will come from. Now you can have some fun with various situations. Put the dog on a Down/Stay and wait for your dog to settle down. Meet the decoy in the center of the field and shake hands. Correct if the dog breaks.

Next, the decoy should stroll away. Turn your back to the decoy. Now have the decoy sneak up on you and grab you from the back. Your dog should immediately come to your aid. If the dog hesitates, the handler should command the dog on what to do. Be careful that you are not positioned between the dog and the decoy, as you could accidentally be bitten. The decoy should always be between the dog and you, and should push you away when the dog bites the decoy.

Attack Out of Bushes or Blind

Take a walk with your dog. Have the decoy hide in a predesignated spot. As you approach, the decoy should jump out at you. The dog should perform the basic routine. The decoy can decide what number of escapes to attempt.

Step 5: Call Offs (Only for Hard Dogs)

A call off is when you send a dog on a bite and at the last second you command "Out." The dog must not bite. Many hard dogs

This dog shows a body bite on entry . . .

followed by an Out and Guard.

The decoy makes a small move and the dog barks a *warning* for the decoy to think about it . . .

The decoy attempts an escape and the dog then bites without hesitation.

require this exercise. It is easily practiced with a long line. Whether you correct with the line or someone else does, the timing is critical. The dog should immediately be called back to the Heel position.

If you have been experiencing difficulties in getting the dog to bite with sufficient intensity, *do not try this exercise.* Such a dog would fold and refuse to bite the next time sent. This dog would be called off easily anyway. Control is not the problem here.

BARK AND HOLD OFF-LEASH

Now that the dog has learned "Search" or "Check," both on the field and at the home or business, we will advance in both areas to the off-leash search.

Step 1

Set up a place for the decoy to hide. A training blind is best, as it is portable and you can place it anywhere you like. Bushes and trees are the next best alternative. Have the decoy make noise and send the dog in on a search. You may have the training director in place, so that if the dog takes a "cheap" bite, you can give a correction with the throw chain.

Step 2

Now we change things on the dog by hiding the decoy in a different blind. On command to search, the dog will run to the blind where the decoy usually hides. If the dog comes up empty, reissue the command. It is acceptable if the decoy needs to make noise in the blind to help the dog the first time. All of your basic Bite-Out-Guard, Reattack and Escorts remain the same. Adjustments are made for the sake of control or confidence as you go along.

AUTOMOBILE PROTECTION—FOLLOWINGS, CARJACKINGS, BREAKDOWNS

Statistics show that one of the more dangerous places for you is in the car. This is because there will be many times when you don't

This dog demonstrates a very intimidating Bark and Hold after finding the hiding suspect.

Photo by Macias

This motorist is much better off waiting for roadside assistance with her Rott-weiler, rather than alone.

This "bad guy" is caught stealing a purse. Situation setups such as this are possible with use of the hidden sleeve.

have control of your own safety. The dangers range from carjackings to drive-by shootings, kidnapping, accidents or breakdowns that could lead to assault, rape or robbery.

There are many times when you cannot control when you may have to stop in a questionable area. You could just be driving through a part of town with a high crime rate, or you may break down at any point along the highway. In any case, the dog is an effective visual deterrent to keep people away from you and your vehicle.

CASE HISTORY

> *A good example of how a K-9 in the car can work to your advantage is Manfred, a Rottweiler. Manfred was riding with his owner in her Jeep on a business trip to downtown Los Angeles. While stopped at a light, his owner found herself suddenly surrounded by a group of young men who were blocking her car and approaching the door. Manfred, who had been lying down sleeping behind the rear seats, was awakened by her yelling "Watch 'em Manfred!" Manfred jumped to his feet and lunged at the man coming toward her door. He let out a roar and hit the window with bared teeth. The man next to the door jumped backward, surprised by the sudden appearance of the 120-pound Rottweiler. The men standing in front of the car made a quick departure and she drove out of the situation a little shaken, but unscathed.*

The dog who is taught to protect the car can also be taught to bite the arm that reaches inside to grab something on the front seat or to grab the owner. This is done with the use of a hidden sleeve or a ring suit jacket. Either of these pieces of equipment will be realistic-looking enough to practice situation setups with the dog.

A full-body suit must be used if the dog is to bite when released from the car. The dog can be released automatically with the use of an automatic bail-out system (door or window opener) for the dog.

The Defense of the Handler. Shown is Nana des Deux Pattois Sch. IA., AD, BH, a Belgian Malinois.

She is shown sitting quietly as the decoy and handler shake hands and converse.

The decoy then circles around to follow the dog and handler. The dog, when told, "On Guard," reverses to the right Heel position, **walking backward.**

When the decoy attempts to strike the handler, the dog moves to apprehend the decoy . . .

. . . in this case biting with a full mouth in the stomach area.

With this device, you can automatically let the dog out if you are assaulted while leaving or approaching your vehicle. These devices come in handy for police officers, K-9 security, private investigators, process servers, repossession agents and others.

The person who is being stalked or targeted for kidnapping must be aware of dangerous areas near his/her home. If you are forced to drive in and out of your property on only one road, be aware that this is a typical place for the stalker to observe or ambush you. Be aware of dangerous areas on your driving route. One-way streets, tunnels, blind corners, areas where the road falls off a hill on one side, or areas where there are excessive amounts of trees or shrubbery blocking your view, are all possible places where you could be blocked by another vehicle and surprised by an attacker.

DON'T BE AN EASY TARGET

Criminals usually rely on their victim's total unawareness to make their jobs easier. Keep track of what vehicles belong in your neighborhood or business locale. If you notice an unusual vehicle—especially if you observe a person sitting inside for any length of time—make a mental note of the car make, model, description of the person(s), and license plate, if you can get close enough. Ask a neighbor to watch this vehicle as well. Many times you can get a better description if the neighbor is watching the person who is watching you, as the stalker's attention is diverted.

Get into the habit of looking in your rearview mirror and taking a mental note of the cars around you. The car that is following you may not be the one directly behind you. Try not to be predictable in your driving routes. This goes for having the dog with you as well. Try not to be predictable so that is harder to target you.

If you think you are being followed, one way to confirm your suspicion is to drive into a residential area that has several exit routes. Make a series of right or left turns that will take you back out to a main road. If someone consistently follows you, they will not realize what you are doing until you end up back at the main road. You may then see the car speed away so that you cannot see the occupants. By making these turns, you are doubling back on yourself, and it is highly unlikely that after three turns someone will also be going your direction.

Security Tips:

1. Be aware of who is around you. Do not get into a vehicle confrontation. Drivers have been known to get into gun play over who had the right-of-way.
2. Do not pull up window to window with questionable-looking characters. Always leave yourself an out—a way to move left, right, etc.
3. If you break down along the highway, take your dog with you to the call box. The dog's main purpose is to protect *you*, not the vehicle.
4. Avoid driving closely behind large trucks or vans that block your view of the road ahead.
5. Try to travel on well-lighted, active streets whenever you have a choice. Avoid known dangerous parts of town, even if it takes extra time.
6. Keep your doors locked, windows up and purse or brief-case on the floor rather than on the seat next to you.

CHAPTER XI

ADVANCED PROTECTION WORK

Because the business security K-9 typically comes in contact with more strangers than the average dog, the training should be molded to each dog's individual job description.

The business owner should take into consideration the work environment as well as the specific use of the K-9. The emphasis should be put on areas of daily use. For instance, if the owner walks down dark streets or alleys on a regular basis, *walking backward at the Heel position* in order to watch the owner's back might be appropriate. On the other hand, if the dog is used only in a store's back room, the owner may consider using a buzzer as a cue for the dog to quickly go into a protection mode.

ELECTRONIC COMMANDS

Like Pavlov's dog, a security dog can be conditioned to respond to a sound stimulus. All you need to do this is to have a panic button connected to a buzzer or bell. After the dog has received full training using the standard voice command, you can move the dog to electronic response.

Dogs are very good at generalizing behaviors. This is also known as *chaining* the dog's training. Run a sequence of events with the buzzer as the beginning sound in the chain. For example: Buzz (sound). Command "Buck, Fass." Buck gets up and runs out, ready to protect. This is done after situation setups have already occurred. After several setups that are initiated by the buzzer, you can drop the voice command altogether. In this case, it is very important that you praise and reward the dog immediately for response to the buzzer.

You can also set up the buzzer for the dog to simply show a defensive mode. Example: *Buzz* (sound). Buck comes running and does a Bark and Hold, or runs out and stops in front of the bad guy, growling and showing teeth.

CASE HISTORY

This show of force worked well for a jewelry store owner. His male Rottweiler was taught to lie quietly out of the way, behind the counter, but was taught to alert on raised voices. A questionable-looking character entered the store one day and began verbally assaulting the owner with ethnic slurs.

The dog, who had been sleeping behind the counter, recognized the sound of a threat, leapt onto the counter next to the cash register and threatened the man at eye level. The perpetrator backed out of the store quickly, apologizing for any misunderstanding.

In this case, the dog was taught that a raised voice was the cue. If the perpetrator had made a quick move, as if reaching for a weapon, the dog had been taught to take him to the ground. We had practiced this scenario over and over again using a muzzle to teach the dog to hit the perpetrator like a lineman and dominate on the ground.

In the same way, we teach reaction to tone by conditioned response. Once given this input, do not expect the dog to adapt to a different action, situation or tone. It is too confusing for the dog to interpret and would require reasoning ability.

DEFENSE OF THE HANDLER—WALKING BACKWARD AT HEEL POSITION

This is a very impressive command for anyone who is watching. The handler is walking along with the dog in the left Heel position, minding his or her own business, when suddenly, out of the shadows, someone appears, walking too close behind the handler for comfort. The handler issues the command "On Guard" to the dog, who moves in front and swings around to the right-hand side of the handler, walking backward, all the while watching the suspect behind the handler. The dog will continue to walk backward, unless the suspect attempts to strike or otherwise touch the handler. The dog has been taught that this is an assault on the handler, which means that the dog can apprehend

To teach this move, you will need to break down the parts of the process for the dog into steps. Later you can chain all of the steps together.

STEP 1

Teach the Dog to Swing from Left to Right

The dog you are working with should already be fully protection trained. Your first step is to teach that "On Guard" means that the dog turns around to focus behind you. This is done by the dog swinging in front of you and turning backward at your right side.

Begin by standing with your back to the decoy, with the dog in the left Heel position. On cue, the decoy should begin to agitate, which will make the dog desire to turn around. Say "On Guard" and slap your right side as you would with the Heel command, then pulling the dog in front of you into the proper position. Praise as soon as the dog is correct. The decoy should then run away. Practice this numerous times and separately from any other step.

STEP 2

Walking Backward

This step is done with three people—the handler, decoy and an assistant trainer who has a long line on the dog as well. The dog must be thoroughly under control on the Out, because of working close to the decoy. The dog may lunge forward to bite at inappropriate times, until the rules of the game are fully learned.

This is the longest part of the process because you are insisting that the dog move backward at a time when the dog desires to move forward *into* the decoy.

Begin with the dog positioned in the backward position on the right side. The decoy should be directly behind the handler—only 2 to 3 feet. The trainer's assistant should be out to the side of the dog and slightly in front of the handler. The assistant is holding a line attached to a training collar. This is not the same collar the handler has. The handler commands the dog "Heel," using the hand signal slap on the *right* thigh. The whole group moves slowly forward. The handler and the assistant give the K-9 some jerks and releases on the training collar until the dog walks backward. This may be only two or three steps the first few times. The decoy's arms should remain casual and at the sides at this point. The dog should receive lavish praise for stepping backward.

It helps if the handler practices the dog moving backward at Heel as an Obedience command as well. The command "Back" can be given. This makes it easier for the dog when a decoy is added as a distraction.

STEP 3

Defend Assault on Handler

This step can be done separately or just after Step 2 is accomplished with some success. The dog must realize not to surge forward toward the decoy *unless* the decoy attempts to assault the handler.

The action here is moving left to right. The trainer's assistant must give tugs and releases that encourage the dog to walk backward.

From the stationary or moving position, the handler only allows the dog to bite when the decoy raises a hand to assault the handler.

To do this, we have the handler calm the dog, while the decoy stands casually at the handler's rear or attempts to approach. On cue, when the decoy attempts to strike the handler, command the dog to bite. This is done first with the handler standing still. Next, the handler, K-9 and decoy move two or three steps forward. Then the decoy attempts the assault.

We now have three steps: (1) On Guard, (2) Walking backward, (3) Defending against assault. Each of these steps is practiced separately until the dog is proficient at each step. It is at this time only, when each step is mastered, that they are put together to perform the defense of the handler routine.

DEFENSE OF THE HANDLER—STATIONARY WITH MOTIONLESS THREAT

Defending the handler can be taught while the handler is in a stationary position as well as when the handler is walking. The handler can teach the dog to swing to the right and watch the handler's back in many situations—on a street corner, at the bank ATM or at a warehouse, dock or other dimly lit place late at night. You can accomplish this quite easily using only Step 1 and a few situation setups.

Very useful is the dog who defends the handler who is sitting in a chair. Wherever you are seated, when told "On Guard," the dog knows that nobody is to touch you. When the dog protects you in a stationary position, it is critical that the dog *be tolerant of anything other than an assault on you.* It is assumed that if you find it necessary to use this command, you are making it clear to the perpetrator that you do not wish to be bothered.

This skill is practiced in setups where the dog should be able to be an inch away from the decoy and not so much as even nip the decoy until the handler is assaulted. In this exercise, the dog should release on request and return to the handler, as the handler's safety is the primary responsibility of the dog.

The handler can teach the dog to swing to the right and watch his or her back in situations such as at this bank ATM.

Using a tree or pole as a support, the handler can confidently sit in a chair while the dog is threatening. This results in the dog learning to threaten without moving forward.

Once the dog under-stands the concept of motionless threat, the handler can hold the leash.

Motionless Threat

Motionless threat is a deterrent in the defense of the handler. This is a talent that dogs can have even if they are not apprehension dogs. There are certain dogs who have a particular talent for motionless threat. This is a command "Alert" or "Pass-auf" where the dog does not move, but rather stands still and issues a threat.

Some dogs will stare and growl, others will snarl and some will bark. This is a very effective deterrent for anyone who has any questions about whether the dog will protect you. The best candidates for this training will naturally make a show vocally or facially in threat training. They are dogs who use a minimal amount of energy jumping up and down and pulling on the leash.

Step 1

Set a chair next to the dog, who is anchored to a tree or post. The length of leash from the post to the dog's collar is only 12 inches. The anchor is attached to the police collar. The handler also has a leash that is attached to the police collar.

Step 2

The decoy must work carefully not to overstress the dog. It is normal for the dog to desire to get up and move toward the decoy. In order to discourage this, the decoy must initiate only the shortest interaction with the dog and reward even the most brief facial displays.

The handler has to be a good coach. The handler should cue the dog by soft tugs on the leash. If the dog begins to move forward, the decoy should break contact, and the handler, without correction, should put the dog back in the Sit position.

Caution: *The handler should never touch the dog while the decoy is agitating.* This overload of input could cause the dog to redirect aggression. When the decoy breaks contact, the handler should soothe the dog by stroking down the dog's back.

Step 3

The dog needs to learn to listen to the handler regarding the appropriate time to threaten. Therefore, the dog's training should involve turning the dog on and off. Each time the dog alerts with a show of teeth, guttural growl or threatening bark, the decoy must run away in order for the dog to feel that the threat caused the decoy to flee.

GUARDING AN OBJECT

The dog guarding an object is a natural instinctive act. Applying human rules to teach the dog not only to guard the object, but also to return automatically to the object when the decoy attempts to drag the dog away, is the most difficult part of the exercise.

STEP 1

Take an object that the dog will defend, such as a toy, ball, puppy tug or puppy sleeve. The dog should be held by the handler on the end of the leash. The decoy should begin to walk in a half circle around the dog and handler, with a hand reaching out as if threatening to take the dog's toy. The decoy should act like a child does when threatening to take another child's toy. As the dog reacts by threatening, standing over the toy, snapping at the decoy and so on, the decoy should jump back as though startled. The handler should praise. The handler gives the dog the command "Guard objét," indicating which object to guard.

STEP 2

After the dog is indicating a clear desire to stand guard over the object, the decoy can wear the Bite Suit. This time when the decoy pretends to be trying to take the toy, he/she will reach in where the dog can bite and make contact. The decoy should make a very obvious movement toward the toy.

When guarding an object, the dog must be aware that a threat can come from anywhere within a 360° radius. The dog must not leave the object.

Using the long line to control the dog's actions, the handler makes sure that the dog stays with the object as the decoy approaches.

When the decoy reaches for the object, the dog is allowed to apprehend.

The decoy, after being bitten, does not fight, but rather slowly backs away. The handler tells the dog to "Out" . . .

. . . and excitedly leads the dog back to the object, patting it and repeating "Guard objét."

The handler then issues the Bite command, "Fass." When the dog bites, the decoy should rise up and freeze for five seconds, allowing the dog to make the decision of whether to let go and return the object or stay with the decoy. If the dog stays with the decoy at this point, the decoy should begin to slowly move sideways or backward, away from the object.

STEP 3

Using the 6-foot leash, the handler should command the dog "Out" (let go) when the dog moves along with the decoy over 10 feet from the object. The handler should excitedly command the dog "Guard objét," and run back to the object, patting it and issuing the command "Guard objét." At this, the decoy, who has been frozen, will begin to move again in a half circle.

STEP 4

After doing the following routine over and over on the 6-foot leash, you can begin to work the dog with the long line. The handler should stand behind the object in order to encourage the dog to return to it. When the dog returns without a correction, you will know you are ready to move to off-leash.

STEP 5

The final step is for the handler to begin to move out of the picture, leaving the dog alone to guard the object and only stepping in to make a correction when the dog makes a mistake.

For the average person, the guard of the object is just a fun exercise to practice under training conditions. Legally, you are not allowed to defend an object with the same force as you would defend a person. In other words, you would never want to leave a bicycle, for instance, outside of a convenience store with the dog "On Guard." This would be a misuse of the training. A security agent, on the other hand, may find this command of some use if

The dog who guards an object must be tolerant of people who are just passing by . . .

. . . even those who might squat down to take a closer look.

But those who try to take the object cannot escape.

the assignment involves protecting a briefcase that holds important documents or money, or if the dog is to protect an important item on an estate property.

Guarding the object is easily transferable to guarding a person, so it is entirely possible that in an emergency situation the handler can tell the dog to guard a person or child.

APPREHENSION THROUGH OBSTACLES AND DISTRACTIONS

You can never really be sure what you and your K-9 may encounter in a real situation. This is why it is important that a business security K-9 is proofed for everything that you can possibly foresee. Using everything that you can think of, for example, gunfire, pots and pans, wadded-up paper to throw at the dog, proof the dog on the training field before the situation setups.

On the training field you can teach the dog to scale walls, jump various obstacles, walk over a catwalk, go through tunnels, around or over barriers and so on. Straw bales are good for making barriers and they are fairly soft so as not to hurt the dog.

HIDDEN SLEEVES AND WEAPON WORK

Hidden sleeves are used to add as much realism to the dog's training as possible. The hidden sleeve allows the decoy to dress in street clothes while working the dog under controlled situations.

When the dog has been trained on a full body bite suit, it is too dangerous for the dog to be worked off-leash. Controlled bites on the leash are entirely possible, as are bites in the house and car where the decoy will offer the arm only through a door or window (see photo, page 193).

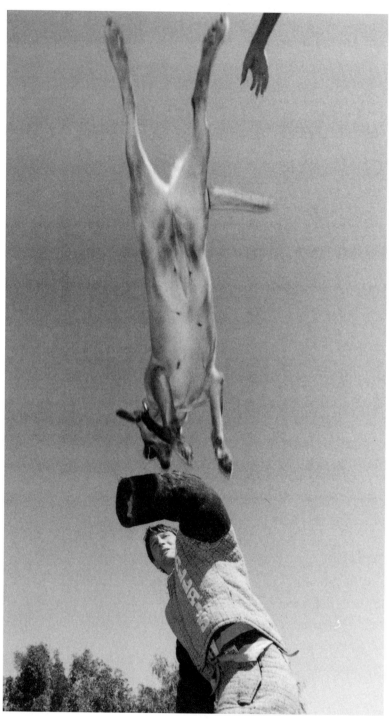

"Nana" demonstrates exceptional courage, leaping from above the decoy.

The weapon should only be shown to the dog in the hand of the arm to be bitten. This can be done with or without the starting pistol firing. If the starting pistol is fired, it should be *before* the dog gets to the decoy. The pistol should always be fired into the air with the muzzle of the gun toward the sky. This is because the sound should be used as a stimulus as well as a distraction. **Note:** You should *never* get into the habit of pointing and firing a pistol with blanks or one that is supposed to be a starting gun. Even a blank gun has muzzle flash and could injure a person or dog. At a close distance, the explosive charge and packing within the firearm is enough to kill a person. **Accidents happen when people assume that the firearm is not dangerous.**

You do not want the dog to be put off by the sound of gunfire, so the sound should be familiar to the dog. This can be done by using a starting pistol frequently in training and taking the dog to an outdoor driving range on a fairly regular basis.

REAR AND SIDE TRANSPORTS

It is necessary to teach a dog to transport a suspect from one place to another. The dog should walk at the handler's Heel position and watch the suspect at all times. If the suspect flees or becomes aggressive, the K-9 apprehends the suspect.

SIDE TRANSPORT

After searching the suspect and removing all weapons from the suspect's possession, the handler will bring the dog up to Heel position at the handler's left and the suspect's right. Escorting the suspect, with the dog in the middle, the dog's attention should be consistently on the suspect.

The exercise in which the decoy attempts to escape is a good foundation, for the dog will have a good focus on the suspect.

The rear transport is the most difficult for the dog, as the K-9 should stay at the handler's Heel while watching the decoy in front of them.

Looking like something from the movie, *Silence of the Lambs,* Ch. Kingsden's Firestorm Dallas models an agitation muzzle used for muzzle attack scenarios.

Rear Transport

The rear transport is as the name implies: transporting the suspect with the dog at the rear position.

After searching the suspect, you simply put the dog in the Heel position on your left side, behind the suspect, and command the suspect to move forward. The dog's attention should be fixed on the suspect so that if he attempts to escape or turns around to fight you, the dog is ready to apprehend again.

MUZZLE ATTACK

Muzzle attack helps to establish realism in training and also helps to build the dog's confidence at the same time. The object is to teach the dog to hit the suspect hard enough to knock the person to the ground and dominate the person.

If the dog can hit the person hard enough just to throw off the aim of a gun or to startle the suspect and make him/her stumble, this can be the difference that keeps the handler alive.

The muzzle used must be made specifically for the purpose of muzzle attack. The muzzle should fit well and completely cover the dog's face. The decoy can now teach the dog to hit a person in street clothes.

Muzzle attack allows the trainers to set up realistic scenarios. For instance, in one jewelry store, the dogs were taught to respond from behind the counters if they heard a raised voice and if they saw the raising of a hand as someone might do if pulling a gun from a pocket or waistband. Muzzle attacks build confidence in the dog. Since the dog is physically dominating the person, a sense of superiority may become evident.

Caution: *This exercise should only be taught to dogs who may face lethal force in a high-risk environment.* This training is done in order to match lethal force with lethal force, and *should only be done under the watchful eye of an experienced professional trainer.*

Ch. Kingsden's Firestorm Dallas demonstrates the proper hitting technique using his chest to knock the man off balance.

Once the man is down, the dog should remain over him, continuing the fight and dominating the perpetrator.

CONVERSION TRAINING

Conversion training is the act of converting the dog from one job description to another. It is fairly common for dogs to be converted from European Sport (Schutzhund, French Ring) to police or security work. Likewise, a personal protection dog may be converted to a business security dog. All that is required is whatever new skills are desired and that the dog be exposed to the required situation setups.

One of the best situations for the business owner is when the dog is utilized at the business and at home. This kind of a relationship helps to ensure that the dog will be present if the handler is attacked. The dog who serves as security for both home and business needs to have situation setups in both places.

If the dog is being converted from Schutzhund to business security, it is imperative that the dog also has good Defense Drive, since this is not emphasized in the Schutzhund dog.

MULTIPLE K-9s

In many situations, the use of two K-9s is necessary. This is typical in property protection or in high-risk situations. K-9s and handlers can work side by side without the dogs ever having to interact with each other, but if they are expected to apprehend a suspect together, they must practice together. It is recommended that only a male and female work as a team. This is because two dogs of the same sex will find it necessary to fight for dominance. They will not typically work well as a team.

Working two K-9s at the same time should be handled carefully. Each dog should have a separate handler and should be put on the decoy separately at first. When the dogs have done this successfully separately many times, each handler may use a long line and give the dog more room to run to the decoy. When the dogs are ready to go off-leash, they should again be brought close to the decoy and

When called out to guard, each dog works as if working alone.

When teaching two dogs to work together, they must be familiar with each other. They must both be well-schooled; and they must first be worked, each with a separate handler.

Working as a team, when properly taught, one dog can go high and the other one low.

placed in the proper area of the suit. When the dogs ultimately are let go from a distance, it is imperative that the decoy have something to take hold of for balance (a tree, a pole), as the dogs may pull in opposite directions. The handlers should be close by and have total voice control over the dogs. *This should never be tried before the dogs have completed and mastered basic off-leash protection exercises.*

CHAPTER XII

SITUATION SETUPS (PRACTICAL EXERCISES)

The key element of successful training for the business security K-9 is situation setups. Remembering that K-9s do not have reasoning ability, situation setups are essential. It is amazing to many people that you can take a dog proficient in police work or Schutzhund sport, and when the same dog is in a home protection role, the dog may not respond properly. This is because the skills of protection have been taught, but the situation to the dog is new. Once this dog understands the rules of the new game, there is no problem. The point is that you want to iron out the possible mistakes before the situation can happen in real life and cause the dog to make a mistake.

BUSINESS SITUATION SETUPS

The place of business where the dog is expected to work should be the site of most situation setups. The threat assessment should be reviewed with the trainer to ensure that the proper exercises are practiced.

Situation setups require practicing from the position in which the dog is used daily.

As stated in Chapter I (under "Your Threat Assessment"), the business owner must visualize the possible scenarios that could happen in his or her business, and plan how the situation should be handled. This means all of the employees of the business should be involved with the drill. A good plan involves the following elements:

1. Deter—How will you deter the criminal? Can you make the criminal decide to go somewhere less secure?
2. Detect—How will you detect the presence of the perpetrator? Will you choose to be silent or vocal about this detection?
3. Distract—If something does occur, do you have an option that will allow you to distract the perpetrator?
4. Defend—Do you have a way to escape? Can you preplan an escape route or construct a safe room? What will you use to defend yourself? A K-9? A firearm? A phone (call for help)? Security system (call for help)? A handler-dog team? Security agent(s)?

Regardless of the methods that you choose to secure your business, you need to be aware of where and when you are vulnerable. Try to minimize this risk as much as possible.

Situations should be set up as realistically as possible. Final details can be ironed out with the handler over the phone, so that the trainer surprises the K-9. Neighboring businesses and police should be warned, as situation setups can look surprisingly realistic to strangers or neighboring businesses who may call the police.

SETUPS USING MULTIPLE K-9s

If more than one dog is to be used, it is imperative that they practice together in the situation as it would be likely to happen. Two

These dogs demonstrate the effectiveness of one dog going high and the other low. The owner can control the dogs by voice from the other side of the counter.

dogs may be used with two different handlers or they may be used as a team. The French have used two dog attack teams for anti-terrorist scenarios. The practice is to teach one dog to hit the legs and the other to hit the upper body. This has the effect of stopping the assailant and taking him to the ground immediately.

When a male and female work together, it is most common for the female to detect an intruder before the male and for the male to bite before the female. Even though this is a stereotype, it has proven true a majority of the time. If more than one security patrol dog is being used, it is wise to work them through practice scenarios together. It is too late when you discover your patrol dog fixating on the other security K-9 when the dog is expected to be apprehending a perpetrator of its own.

SETUPS USING OBSTACLES, DISTRACTIONS, WEAPONS AND HIDDEN SLEEVES

In business, anything goes. You and your dog may encounter anything! For example, we know of a business owner who was set up and killed during the holidays by a man dressed as Santa Claus. Although we do not suggest dressing up the decoy like Santa Claus or teaching your dog to attack Santa, our point is that almost anything is possible. More probable scenarios such as the perpetrator throwing something at your dog, luring the dog with food, trying to intimidate or sweet-talk the dog are all very real possibilities.

OBSTACLES

Be aware of the obstacles your dog may need to comfortably negotiate in your business. If the dog is expected to jump over a counter, then practice this in training. If the dog is expected to open a swinging gate or dodge around merchandise in pursuit of a suspect, then this must be practiced. In real life, when a human is being pursued by another person or K-9, it is common for this person to attempt to knock things over in the path of the pursuer in order to buy some time. This should also be practiced.

Another common maneuver is for the suspect to attempt to hide in the place of business. This could be in a closet, above the ceiling, under a table, under a piece of overturned furniture, and so on. Practice these scenarios so that you will know how to respond in a real situation. Remember that slippery surfaces are also obstacles; they are not easy for a K-9 to traverse. The K-9 must be trained on them in case this is where the K-9 is standing in a real situation.

DISTRACTIONS

The biggest distractions to a dog are ones that trigger the dog's instincts. The cause is typically a smell or a sound, but it can also be sight. If the dog is conditioned to react properly, you must be as ready as you can be, even in the presence of the following distractions: a hunger reaction (food smells), breeding reaction (female in season), territorial behavior (scent marking), fear or startle reaction (loud noise), quick movement (Prey Drive, prey chasing).

Distractions are difficult to proof because you are working against the dog's instincts. The best you can do is to try and foresee the distractions. Try to avoid the problem and to minimize the result of the conflict.

For example, you can minimize the use of the female in season against your male dog by not using him as a stud dog. This does not mean that a dog who has not bred will ignore a bitch in season, but he will not be *as distracted*. It is proven that once a stud dog is conditioned to receive bitches, the scent will kick in conditioned response and you will have a dog with a one-track mind!

POISON PROOFING

Proofing the dog against food is a greater necessity. A protection dog who turns into a pussycat when offered food is ineffective.

It is imperative that you build poison proofing into the business

Teaching the dog to apprehend from a car, out of a window or door, is a good idea for a traveling personal protection K-9.

The dog should stay on the man when he goes down. The handler never calls the dog out without having control when the decoy is down.

security K-9's training if the dog is ever expected to work alone. With a human handler by the dog's side, it is doubtful that anyone would attempt to poison the dog. However, if your K-9 is expected to protect an area, livestock, a vehicle or a yard, you cannot rule out the possibility of intentional poisoning.

You can poison-proof your dog using three methods: 1) Obedience, food refusal; 2) food agitation, protection; 3) electric shock, food association from ground and decoy. Your dog should learn food refusal first as an Obedience exercise. This establishes the first idea in the dog's mind that taking food from a stranger is not allowed. The exercise is conducted by following these steps:

1. The handler puts the dog on a Down/Stay and moves to the Heel position.
2. The trainer's assistant then moves toward the dog and handler with a bag of goodies (hot dogs, chicken nuggets), and begins to offer the goodies to the dog.
3. The handler talks to the dog and gives positive and negative feedback as required, with a verbal "good dog, good Down/Stay." The dog opens its mouth toward the food. "No" is given, quick and sharp. At this point, a quick jerk on the collar may be required with some dogs. Others will require only a verbal correction. As the dog learns not take food from the hand, you can move on to the next step.
4. The assistant now starts to toss bits of food near the dog. The toss should gradually be as close to the dog as possible.
5. The handler corrects and praises as required. If possible, the handler can begin to step away from the dog.
6. The next time the handler will start at a distance of 6 feet and begin to verbally praise and correct the dog as needed. With each exercise, the handler will get farther and farther away.
7. The assistant now approaches directly and begins to toss tidbits of food near the dog. Eventually, the handler will be out of sight, behind a blind or around a corner.

PROTECTION (AGITATING WITH FOOD)

In order to form a negative conditioned response toward a stranger offering food, we must agitate with food. This refers back to the idea of "chaining events." The dog who sees a person approaching the fence offering food must associate this action with agitation.

WEAPONS

The business security K-9 needs to learn that the sight of weapons coupled with aggressive overtones means instant response is necessary. Gunfire should not spook the dog. In fact, it should trigger an aggressive response toward the shooter. This is accomplished by shooting a starting pistol at the onset of protection work.

During the process of protection training, various sticks have been used and by now the dog should take stick hits without flinching. *Stick hits are placed on the dog not to hurt the dog, but to teach the dog to disregard the hits rather than stop the bite.*

The business owner must consider all of the potential weapons that may be used by an intruder. No, the K-9 cannot be expected to win against a .357 Magnum, but the dog can deter, distract, detect and defend long enough to possibly save your life.

HIDDEN SLEEVES

Hidden sleeves can be used for realism. The idea is to make the arm look as realistic as possible to the dog. The decoy still requires protection from the bite. When a K-9 knows how to give a full body bite, the work with a hidden sleeve must be done carefully. The best areas to use hidden sleeves are small and enclosed, such as in the car (through the window) or over a counter or desk.

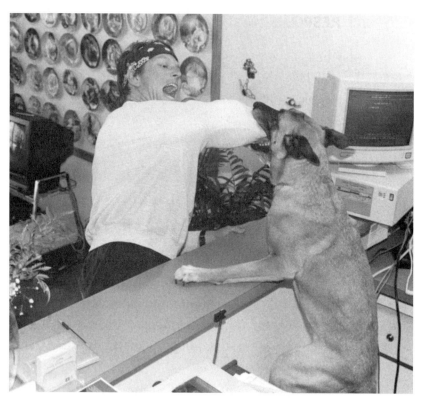

Hidden sleeves should be used for realism. This equipment allows the dog to learn on a decoy in street clothes.

"Nana" demonstrates the defense of the handler on a downtown street.

INSTANT RESPONSE WITH USE OF MUZZLES

One of the best ways to practice for realism is muzzle attack. Muzzle attack allows the dog to attack a person in street clothes without being able to bite. The object is to teach the dog to use its body to knock down *and* dominate the perpetrator.

The dog should get used to wearing the muzzle prior to this training. One of the easiest ways to do this is to put on the muzzle and practice the Heel exercise. When the dog achieves even the smallest success, lavish praise should be given along with a food reward in some cases.

Once the dog is comfortable with the muzzle, it is time to set up situations. For instance, in a jewelry store, the decoy may come in looking like a typical customer, looking into the cases at the jewelry. The decoy may ask, "Do you have any gold chains?" The store owner can then show the decoy the gold chains while holding a conversation. At some point, the decoy steps back and produces a gun, yelling, "All right, nobody move!" As this happens, the dog should be cued to attack. Whether by the decoy's actions, an electronic signal or a verbal command, the dog should be trained over and over again in scenarios such as this in order to know how to respond.

It is not unusual in the beginning to have to tell the K-9 how to respond. After a while, the K-9 begins to generalize the situation and react without the cue.

SETUPS FOR MOTIONLESS THREAT

Motionless threat is useful in certain situations. When a dog can threaten on command without moving, the K-9 looks incredibly well trained and under control. It also prevents the necessity of needing all the handler's strength to hold the dog. People who are partially disabled benefit greatly from a dog who has this skill.

Situation setups can be done from behind a counter, sitting in a chair or from your car. In much the same way as the muzzle attack, motionless threat should be set up with the decoy approaching as an average person, maybe even talking to you and the dog. The dog should be subtly cued. If the dog responds, the decoy should make a quick exit, thereby rewarding the dog's behavior. If the dog fails to react, the decoy should become obviously aggressive to the dog and handler until the dog reacts properly.

STREET WORK FOR DEFENSE OF THE HANDLER

The defense of the handler exercise can be practiced in a variety of environments such as a park, city street or dark alley. The decoy walks behind the dog and handler for some distance. The handler gives the command "On Guard" when the decoy closes to 6 feet behind the team. The dog should swing from the left Heel position to the right Heel position. At this point, the dog continues to walk backward at the Heel position, watching the person who is following. If the follower moves to touch or grab the handler, the dog may then apprehend the follower.

A shorter version of this command can be practiced from a stationary position. At an ATM or on a street corner, the dog can be put "On Guard" to watch the owner's back side

STREET WORK FOR GUARDING THE HANDLER OR OBJECT

Guarding the handler takes motionless threat to a different level. With one command, the dog can be told not to allow anyone to touch the handler. This should be done in areas that are frequented

Told to "Guard objét," Nana will not allow this questionable-looking character to take the purse or briefcase.

Muzzle attack practice sessions prepare the dog for real encounters.

by the owner. This command is particularly handy when the job invites a great deal of harassment, such as those in the entertainment field. For many of these people, the K-9 is not only a deterrent, but a bodyguard as well.

Guarding an object should *only* be done with the dog in a secure place. This would mean in a fenced area, in a vehicle, on a leash and so on.

An example of a situation setup for object protection would be a dog protecting a briefcase. The handler walks up to a counter in a business place, such as a hotel, and places the briefcase next to the dog, commanding "On Guard." At this point, the decoy should approach and attempt to take the briefcase. This can be done both directly and more subtly. The decoy should also walk up and do nothing. This is so that the dog does *not* become conditioned to *always* expect an attempt.

■ ■ ■

Guarding the object can also be practiced with a muzzle. This allows the decoy to conduct this exercise in street clothes.

Caution: *All of the setups described in this section should be conducted with the guidance of a professional trainer.* The scenarios described here are intricate to teach and, if taught improperly, could adversely affect the dog's ability to work effectively. The authors caution the reader not to attempt this type of training without professional assistance.

CHAPTER XIII

THE BUSINESS SECURITY K-9
—A TRUE STORY

Ed and Marsha Schlesinger owned a family-operated jewelry store in a Southern California shopping center. They had always been an animal-oriented family and had owned several dogs and horses over the years. They had never considered taking their dogs to the store with them . . . until the day that they were robbed, tied up, held at gunpoint and forced to open the safe and empty its contents. Insurance covered the loss of merchandise, but the Schlesingers quickly realized that their lives could have been lost as well.

Enter Lizzy and Luke, their Rottweilers. After receiving professional training required to understand their jobs and take them seriously, the dogs become everyday fixtures in the store. We advised the Schlesingers to keep the dogs out of traffic areas, keeping at least one under the jewelry cases so that this dog would surprise a would-be perpetrator. Keeping the other behind the cashier's counter also provided a more than adequate deterrent. The dogs were then trained to respond to raised voices or tension with barks and growls. Physical moves such as reaching over the counter or pulling a weapon from a jacket resulted in the dog's using physical force. Muzzle attack had been practiced for this purpose.

One day, as Luke lay behind the counter and Lizzy under the jewelry case, two perpetrators entered the store. In typical fashion, one stayed by the door and the other headed straight to the cash register. This man came to an abrupt halt as he saw a 130-pound Rottweiler staring at him. His eyes bulged and he said, "Oh ——! That's a huge dog!" At the same time, the perpetrator at the back door of the store heard a low growl coming from under the jewelry counter. He also said, "Oh ——! There's another one over here!" The perpetrator at the counter took a step back and began to pull something out of his pocket. Upon seeing this move, Luke jumped up and leaped over the counter. Screaming with terror, the two would-be assailants fled with the dogs in close pursuit. The dogs halted at the door. The men never showed their faces in the store again.

It should be noted that these dogs were in this store day in and day out for years—with adults and children coming and going—without even a growl or aggressive act. When the two perpetrators came along, however, both the dogs and the Schlesingers instinctively knew that these two goons were up to no good. There was no need for a bite. The dogs proved that a strong deterrent can prevent an incident from happening.

This story is a prime example of how a business security K-9 can blend into the workplace and be useful in case of a confrontation.

It is people like the Schlesinger family, who are already animal lovers, who fit perfectly into the handler role with the Business Security K-9 ever present as an integral part of their daily lives.

CHAPTER XIV

CONCLUSION

If this were a perfect world, we could live without fear of being victimized or violated by others. But, this is not a perfect world, as we are well aware. Today we pray for peace, but it is wise to plan for our protection. This is a much wiser act than to plan for peace and find ourselves praying for our lives.

Throughout history, the dog has served in whatever capacity was necessary for our survival. People and dogs have a symbiotic relationship. Today we find dogs working in many job situations: as rescue dogs for disaster victims; in arson, explosives and narcotics detection; in Seeing Eye work and as dogs for the disabled or hearing impaired; as police SWAT and anti-terrorist K-9s and, of course, as home and family protection dogs and business security K-9s.

The dog does not care whether the owner is a prince or pauper, a corporate CEO or the owner of a small shop. The dog will protect all with the same love, devotion and loyalty to the death, if necessary.

Missouri State Senator George Graham Vest wrote this "Tribute to the Dog" in 1870:

The one absolutely unselfish friend a person can have in this selfish world, the one that never proves ungrateful or treacherous, is a dog.

GLOSSARY OF TERMS

Agitate/Agitation: Bringing out the dog's courage and Defense and Prey drives at the appropriate times.

Agitation stick: A stick made of nylon, padded or nonpadded, bamboo reed or popper. It can be used to make noise or to lightly tap the dog in training.

AKC show: American Kennel Club show, typically involving Conformation or Obedience. Tracking, Herding, Coursing and hunting competitions are held independently of Conformation or Obedience.

Basic Obedience commands: "Heel," "Sit," "Down," "Come" and "Stay" learned both on and off leash.

"Bite" command: Command to apprehend a person. "Fass" in German.

Cervical Vertebral Instability (CVI) or Wobblers: Generally occurs in older males, caused by pinched nerves in the rear end of the dog. This is genetic and the dog is unsuitable for breeding. (Ref: Dr. Beckie Williams, DVM & GSD Breeder.)

Champion: A dog that through competition in the breed ring has earned enough points to be named champion. This requires 15 points under at least three judges, including at least two wins of 3, 4 or 5 points.

"Check" command: Command to check the house or search for intruders.

Choke chain/training collar: Collar that tightens when a correction is applied and releases to a loose position when the dog is correctly under command.

Conformation: The anatomical makeup of the dog judged for correctness of structure and type according to a breed Standard of perfection.

Controlled aggression: The act of making the dog aggressive but *not* mean (obedient aggression); at the same time teaching to cease aggression on command.

Defense Drive: The drive to protect territory, self, owner or property.

Desensitized: To lessen sensitivity through experience.

European bite suit: The full body suit designed in Europe for maximum movement with maximum protection for the decoy.

Fear-aggressive: A dog that is aggressive because he/she is afraid. The dog shows the body language of fear, i.e., tail tucked, eyes rolled back, hackles up, etc., while acting aggressive.

Fetch: To retrieve an article.

"Gib Laut": "Speak" command. German command to bark.

Handler: The person who holds the dog and coaches the dog into the proper actions.

Hip Dysplasia: A primarily genetic disorder in the ball and socket of the hip joint that can result in lameness and early onset of severe arthritis.

"Hold" command: A command to guard the person silently or with a bark and hold.

Light leash: A light Toy breed leash.

Long line: A 30-foot leash.

Muzzle: A device worn on the face that will not allow the dog to bite.

"Out" command: Command used to cease aggression whenever necessary. The dog must obey the owner and remain calm.

Parvovirus: An intestinal virus that is potentially fatal.

Pet quality: A pup or adult that, because of one or more faults or deviations from the Standard, should not be bred.

Police collar: A 2-inch-wide leather collar used for protection.

Prey Drive: The drive that causes the dog to chase and bite at prey.

Prong collar: Collar that pinches neck at several points.

Puppy gate/Baby gate: Gate used in doorways to hold or keep the pup out of a specific area.

Puppy tug: A device made of rolled burlap used to teach the dog to bite properly by using techniques involving play.

Recessive genes: Inherited characteristics that are not obvious in a given dog, but that may be passed on to offspring.

Ring sport: French dog sport involving Obedience, Agility and protection exercises.

Safety collar: An extra collar worn in case equipment breaks.

Schutzhund: German dog sport involving Obedience, Tracking and protection exercises.

Sleeves: Protection equipment worn on the arm only. Used to teach the dog to bite with a full mouth.

Socialization: Making sure that the dog is comfortable around adults, children and other animals.

"Stand" command: Teaching the dog to stand for examination for practical purposes, Obedience or show.

Tab/Handle: A 6–10-inch leash or handle.

Titled: A degree earned through competition in a specifically regulated activity.

Training director: The most knowledgeable person who directs the action between the decoy, handler and dog.

Von Willebrand's disease: A free-bleeding disorder that is inherited.

"Watch 'em" or "Pas-Auf" command: Command for dog to be alert.

SECURITY TERMINOLOGY

Advance: Checking the security and readiness of the area in advance of the principal's (client's) arrival.

Back way trip: Principal is brought in through a side or back door.

CCTV: Closed-circuit TV. Allows the business owner to record and observe activities in the business.

Coded trip: A job in which the protectors and principals communicate in code.

Detector cell: A detector that can be placed under any object likely to be stolen, e.g., typewriter, computer, etc. When the object is moved, the cell is activated.

Infrared: Sensors that detect body heat within a protected area.

Loose job: Low threat level.

Motion detectors: Sensors set strategically in an area to pick up and alert security to movement within the protected area.

Parade: Instance in which a client is making an entrance (on display) in front of a crowd.

Perpetrator: The person from whom the principal is being protected.

Person Protection Specialist (PPS): Title earned through school to be a professional bodyguard. Personal Protection Specialist is the correct title.

Principal: The client (VIP).

Scam trip: Principal is incognito. May be brought in a bread truck, disguise, etc., to trick the perpetrator.

Security mirror: Two-way mirror that allows the business owner to view the customers without the customers knowing.

Threat assessment: The conclusion of the risk assessed by looking at all of the elements of threat.

Tight job: High threat level.

VIP: Very important person.

SUGGESTED READING

Bamberger, Michelle, DVM. *Help! A Quick Guide to First Aid for Your Dog*. New York: Howell Book House, 1993.

Barwig, Susan, and Stewart Hilliard. *Schutzhund—Theory and Training Methods*. New York: Howell Book House, 1991.

Campbell, Dr. William. *Behavior Problems in Dogs*. Santa Barbara, CA: American Veterinary Publications, Inc., 1991.

Carlson, Delbert G., DVM, and James M. Giffin, MD. *Dog Owner's Home Veterinary Handbook*. New York: Howell Book House, 1992.

Duet, Karen Freeman and George Duet. *The Home & Family Protection Dog: Selection and Training*. New York, Howell Book House, 1992.

Fox, Michael. *Understanding Your Dog*. New York: Coward, McCann, and Geoghegan, 1992.

Kobetz, Dr. Richard W., DPA. *Providing Executive Protection*. Executive Protection Institute.

Lanting, Fred L. *Canine Hip Dysplasia*. Loveland, CO: Alpine Publications, Inc.

Pffaffenberger, Clarence. *The New Knowledge of Dog Behavior.* New York: Howell Book House, 1963.

Saunders, Blanche. *The Complete Book of Dog Obedience.* New York: Howell Book House, 1978.

Strickland, Winifred. *Expert Obedience Training for Dogs.* New York: Macmillan, 1988.

Whitney, Leon, DMV. *Dog Psychology.* New York: Howell Book House, 1971.

INDEX

Adult dogs
  advantages, 101
  from animal shelters, 74–75
  bonding process with, 102, 104
  with children, 102
  disadvantages, 102
  training costs, 102
Aggression
  ceasing on command, 165
  predisposition toward, 5–6, 55,
    57–58
  stabilizing, 177
  toward owners, 83, 166–67
  untrained, 166
Agility work, 142, 160
  situation setups, 227–28
Agitating Outs, 171–72
Agitation, friendly, 171
Agitation sticks, 163, 179
Airline travel, 154
Akitas, 90, 91–92
Alarm dogs, 19
  breeds suited to, 85

size considerations, 21–22, 72
temperaments suited to,
  20
Alarm systems
  backup power sources, 12, 43
  features, 13
  silent, 44, 46, 47
  used in dog training, 44, 199–200
Alert command, 168, 207
Allergies, 2, 17, 85
Alpha personalities, 23, 57, 111
American Staffordshire Terriers, 90, 92
Anchoring the dog, 129
Animal shelters as sources for dogs,
  74–75
Apartment complex security patrols,
  32–33
Apartments, dogs suitable for, 86
Apprehension work
  attack practice, 190
  bark and hold practice, 186–88,
    192
  body bites, 188

ABOUT THE AUTHORS

George and Karen Duet own and operate Kingsden's Kennel and K-9 Companions Dog Training Co. Together with their associates and training staff they provide training for all breeds in problem-solving, Obedience and home manners. They specialize in training dogs of sound temperament in the art of personal protection and home and business security. K-9 Companions has branches in Los Angeles, Orange County, Riverside, and San Diego, California. They are also the authors of *The Home and Family Protection Dog* (Howell, 1993).

The Duets' backgrounds include experience in American Kennel Club Obedience Trials and conformation shows, German Schutzhund and French Ring Sport training, as well as U.S. Army training. George Duet retired from the Army after 20 years' service, and spent time as Kennel Master in Fort Benning, Georgia, and now also teaches the use of firearms to men and women. He is a distinguished pistol shot and was the Chief Sniper Instructor for the U.S. Army in Vietnam as well as the coach of the U.S. Army shooting team, pistol division.

The Duets also provide protective services for VIPs in the form of handler-dog teams or protective agents on an on-call basis. They both hold the title of Personal Protection Specialist (P.P.S.) awarded by the Executive Protection Institute, Berryville, Virginia. They are members of Nine Lives Associates, an international network of personal protection specialists and are pioneering the field of K-9 security in the role of executive protection and estate protection

The Duets are working with trainers and breeders to educate the public in K-9 management and training. They believe with proper breeding and training regulations, unwarranted attacks by all dogs can be drastically reduced.